KETO
MEAL PREP
The Complete Guide for Beginners
`21 Days Keto Meal Plan`

PETER BRAGG

Legal & Disclaimer

The information contained in this book and its contents is not designed to replace or take the place of any form of medical or professional advice; and is not meant to replace the need for independent medical, financial, legal or other professional advice or services, as may be required. The content and information in this book have been provided for educational and entertainment purposes only.

The content and information contained in this book have been compiled from sources deemed reliable, and it is accurate to the best of the Author's knowledge, information, and belief.

However, the Author cannot guarantee its accuracy and validity and cannot be held liable for any errors and/or omissions. Further, changes are periodically made to this book as and when needed.

Where appropriate and/or necessary, you must consult a professional (including but not limited to your doctor, attorney, financial advisor or such other professional advisor) before using any of the suggested remedies, techniques, or information in this book.

Upon using the contents and information contained in this book, you agree to hold harmless the Author from and against any damages, costs, and expenses, including any legal fees potentially resulting from the application of any of the information provided by this book. This disclaimer applies to any loss, damages or injury caused by the use and application, whether directly or indirectly, of any advice or information presented, whether for breach of contract, tort, negligence, personal injury, criminal intent, or under any other cause of action.

You agree to accept all risks of using the information presented inside this book.

You agree that by continuing to read this book, where appropriate and/or necessary, you shall consult a professional (including but not limited to your doctor, attorney, or financial advisor or such other advisor as needed) before using any of the suggested remedies, techniques, or information in this book.

Table of Contents

DESCRIPTION 10

INTRODUCTION 12

KETO EXPLAINED...13

BENEFITS OF KETO DIET 23

21 DAYS MEAL PLAN................................... 30

BREAKFAST RECIPES 35

Savory Cheddar Pancakes................................ 36

Chia Cinnamon Vanilla Granola...................... 38

Cheese and Sausage in Portobello Breakfast Burgers 40

Cheese Keto Quiche 42

Raspberries Breakfast Scones 44

Cinnamon Coconut Porridge 46

Easy Scotch Eggs 48

Easy Breakfast Tacos...................................... 50

Bacon and Ricotta Breakfast Muffins 52

Keto Mini Waffles 54

Creamy Herbed-Baked Eggs 56

Vanilla Smoothie 60

Blackberry Egg Bake 62

Chocolate Chip Waffles 66

Chocolate and Peanut Butter Muffins 68

Butter Coffee 70

Mocha Chia Pudding 72

Keto Green Eggs 74

Cheddar Souffles 76

Ricotta Pie 78

LUNCH RECIPES **81**

Savory Beef Balls with Asian Style Dip 82

Chicken Curry with Oil-Roasted Peanuts 84

Zucchini Beef Lasagna 86

Chicken Bell Pepper Kebabs 88

Easy Grilled Shrimp with Avocado, Tomato and
Onion Salad 90

Balsamic Herbed Pork Tenderloin 92

Keto Squash-getti with Herbed Meatballs............. 94

Sardine and Garden Salad 98

Herbed Parmesan Chicken Fingers 100

Ham, Onion and Green Bean Salad 102

Cheesy Avocado Beef Patties...............................104

Cheesy Sausage, Mushroom and Spaghetti Squash Casserole 106

Keto Cubano 110

Pork Salad 112

Baked Chicken Nuggets 114

Salmon and Potato Salad 118

Lamb Spinach Rogan Josh 120

Keto Pork and Plums...122

Chili Orange Shrimp 124

Vegetable Wraps 126

Collard Greens and Bacon 128

DINNER RECIPES.. **131**

Deviled Eggs with Chopped Bacon 132

Fried Cheesy Avocado Wedges 136

Simple Beef Chili 138

Low Carb Hearty Pot Roast.................................140

Roasted Garlic Butter Cod with Bok Choy 142

Creamy Chicken Soup 144

Ginger Sesame Halibut.......................................146

Goat Cheese and Smoked Onion Pizza..................148

Savory Butternut Squash Soup............................150

Super Green Soup 152

Bacon Burgers...154

Italian Meatballs...156

Garlic Pork Chops 162

Spaghetti Carbonara 164

Shrimp Tuscany 166

Sea Bass...168

Eggs and Bacon...170

Chicken and Sprout Bake...................................172

SNACKS/DESSERTS **175**

Avocado, Cream Cheese and Cucumber Bites 176

Ham 'n' Cheese Puffs 178

Walnut Parmesan Bites 180

Cream Cheese Bacon Stuffed Jalapenos 182

Low Carb Guacamole 184

Smoked Salmon and Dill Spread 186

Coco Lime Fat Bombs..188

Choco Peanut Fat Bombs 190

Chocolate Coated Bacon 194

Cinnamon Butter...198

Roasted Eggplant Spread 200

Bacon Mozzarella Sticks 206

Coconut Milk Ice Cream.......................................208

Coconut Macaroons 210

Raspberry Pops..212

Avocado Tropical Treat 214

Keto Lava Cake 216

Apple Detox..218

Mango Smoothie 220

CONCLUSION **223**

KETO MEAL PREP

Description

Do you desire to have good health? Nutritional ketosis, the process by which the body burns fat rather than sugar for fuel, is an effective approach to radically improving health. This is achieved by eating a high-fat, low-carbohydrate, moderate-protein diet.

This book aims to give you both a test subject to study and demonstrate the effects of the Ketogenic diet, a ready-to-go nutritious meal plan for 21 days to easily kick-start your journey, but also to offer you a much more targeted and selective source of information with respect to what you can find in other books.

It is known that what's best for one's health is restricting dietary fat and consuming lots of carbohydrates, especially "healthy whole grains." But the truth, as proven by different medical studies, is that eating more fat and fewer carbs are beneficial for the treatment of a wide range of health problems. It can help you lose weight, increase energy, stabilize blood sugar, improve mental focus, balance hormones, and much more.

You can use the book as a guide to help get you started on your way should you be unfamiliar with this low carb diet, or if you are just off it for a while and in need of a specific plan to help you along the way.

With the strategies and recipes you'll find here, you can end food obsession, cravings, and restrictions through sound nutrition practices and delicious whole food meals so that you can get the weight and health you want without self-loathing or guilt.

Introduction

I hope this book helps you with your weight loss efforts. This cookbook is an in-depth guide on how to embrace and introduce the Keto diet into your life.

I have provided you with some of the best Keto recipes to follow on a daily basis for a period of 21 days. This guide is designed to introduce you to the Keto diet and walk you through what is to be expected while on the Keto diet. This book contains a variety of recipes that will satisfy even the most selective eaters! There is a recipe for everyone!

In this book, readers will discover the 21 days full plan delicious recipes. The recipes utilize chicken, cheese, pork, soups, fish/seafood, vegetables and spices among other ingredients.

With all the information in this book, you should be well on your way to building your Keto diet meal prep plan and having a healthier lifestyle with the Keto diet.

Keto Explained

The ketogenic diet causes ketone bodies to be produced by your liver, thus shifting your body's metabolism away from using glucose as the primary source of fuel and toward fat utilization. To accomplish this, the ketogenic diet restricts carbohydrate intake below a certain level – usually 100 grams per day. The daily amount depends on your health and weight loss goals.

How Does the Ketogenic Diet Work?

We all know that we need food for energy. On a typical high-carb diet, your body specifically uses glucose as the primary source of energy; it is easier for your body to convert carbs to glucose than it is with other types of energy sources.

Insulin will also be produced to process the glucose in your bloodstream, and the fats will get stored by the body, eventually piling up and causing a litany of health problems.

The ketogenic diet enables your body to use another energy source for fuel; the concept is that with a lower carb intake, you will be depriving your body of the glucose it needs and will make use of the fats instead, as it falls into a state known as ketosis.

Ketosis is a natural state of the body wherein the liver will break down the available fats instead of glucose or carbohydrates, and ketones will be produced which will then be burned by the body as the primary energy source, Your goal with the ketogenic diet is to force your body into this metabolic state.

Your body is designed to adapt to a metabolic state easily, so you only need to worry about following the diet and let your body handle the rest.

The ketogenic diet is different from other low-carb diets. The difference is that your diet should be about 70-75 percent of calories from fat, 20-25 percent from protein, and 5-10 percent from carbohydrates each day.

If you follow these guidelines, your diet will be composed of high-fats and moderate protein intake, and there will be no need to count calories

Protein is limited because it affects the insulin and blood sugar in your body.

If you consume protein in large quantities, the excess gets converted to glucose. As a result, your body will not reach a state of ketosis Have you ever come to note that whenever you have a food craving, you usually go for carb-rich foods? That's because your brain has labeled the starchy and sweet foods as comfort foods. Our main goal with the ketogenic diet is to drastically reduce the intake of carbohydrates and choose a healthier alternative.

In theory, if you limit your carb intake and achieve a state of ketosis, the excess weight will be shed easily.

How to know when you are in Ketosis

Whether you have taken any tests to discover your ketosis status, your body will exhibit physical signs to prompt you. You may have a loss of appetite, increased thirst, have bad breath, or notice a stronger urine smell. These are all clues from your body.

Ketosis and Your Sleep Patterns

After you have a good night of sleep, your body is in ketosis since you have been in a fasted state for 8 hours or more, you are on the way to burning ketones. If you are new to the high-fat and low-carb dieting, the optimal fat-burning state takes time. Your body has depended on bringing in carbs and glucose; it will not readily give up carbs and start to crave saturated fats. The restless night is also a normal side effect. Vitamin supplements can sometimes remedy the problem that can be caused by a lowered insulin and serotonin level. For a quick fix; try one-half of a tablespoon of fruit spread and a square of chocolate.

Bad Breath Happens

You may notice a metallic or fruity taste with an odor similar to nail polish remover. This is the by-product of acetoacetic acid (acetone) that is an obvious indication. You may also experience a drier mouth. These changes are normal as a side effect as your body processes these high-fat foods.

Once you are accustomed to the Ketogenic dieting techniques, the bad breath symptoms will pass. If you are socializing, try a diet soda or a no-sugar drink. Sugar-free gum is also a quick fix. Always check the nutrition labels for carbohydrate facts; you may be surprised. These are not allowed on the Keto diet because they reduce ketones. Therefore, only use it temporarily. If you are at home, just grab the toothbrush.

Lowered Appetite

When you reduce your carbs and proteins, you will be increasing your fat intake. The reduced appetite comes from the multitude of fibrous veggies, fats, and satiating nutrients provided in the new diet.

The "full" factor is a huge benefit to the Ketogenic plan. It will give you one less thing to worry about—being hungry.

Thirst is increased

Fluid retention is increased when you are consuming carbohydrates.

Once the carbs are flushed away, water weight is lost. You counterbalance by increasing the water intake since you are probably dehydrated.

The Keto diet calls for one to have more water intake because you are storing carbs. If you are dehydrated, your body can use the stored carbs to restore hydration.

When you're in ketosis, the carbs are removed, and your body doesn't have the water reserves. If you have tried other diets, you might have been dehydrated, but the higher carbohydrate counts stopped you from being thirsty.

Thus, the Keto state is a diuretic state, so drink plenty of water daily.

Digestive Issues

With the sudden change in diet; it's expected you may have problems including constipation or diarrhea when you first start the Keto diet. Individuals are different, and variation may rely on the foods you decide to eat to increase your fiber intake using various vegetables.

You may experience issues because your fiber intake may be too high in comparison to your previous diet. Try reducing certain "new" foods until the transitional phase of Keto is concluded. It should clear up with time.

You may be lacking beneficial bacteria. Try consuming fermented foods to increase your probiotics and aid digestion. You can benefit from B vitamins, omega-3 fatty acids, and beneficial enzymes as well.

Other Possible Side Effects

Induction Flu: The diet can make you irritable, nauseous, a bit confused, lethargic, and possibly suffer from a headache.

Several days into the plan should remedy these effects. If not, add one-half of a teaspoon of salt to a glass of water and drink it to help with the side effects. You may need to do this once a day for about the first week, and it could take about 15 to 20 minutes before it helps. It will go away!

Constipation: During the Ketogenic plan you must drink plenty of water, or you could easily become constipated because of dehydration.

The low carbs contribute to the issue. Eat the right veggies and add a small amount of salt to your food to help with the movements. If all else fails, try some *Milk of Magnesia.*

Leg Cramps: The loss of magnesium (a mineral) can be a demon and create a bit of pain with the onset of the Keto diet plan changes. With the loss of the minerals during urination, you could experience bouts of cramps in your legs.

Heart Palpitations: You may begin to feel "fluttery" as a result of dehydration or because of an insufficient intake of salt. Try to make adjustments, but if you don't feel better quickly, you should seek emergency care.

The Health Benefits of the Ketogenic Diet

1. Faster & sustainable weight loss

Cutting carbs is the fastest and surest way to lose weight quickly.

First, a low-carb diet, such as the Ketogenic diet, gets rid of all the excess water from your body. You will notice that there is a loss of water weight.

Additionally, since the Keto diet lowers your insulin levels, your kidneys start shedding the excess sodium which leads to rapid weight loss within the first two weeks

For as long as you remain committed to the Ketogenic diet, you will continue losing weight until you achieved your ideal weight

2. *Slimmer waistlines*

Not all the fat in your body is the same. Where the fat is stored in your body is what will determine how your weight affects your health. There is subcutaneous fat which is stored under the skin and visceral fat that is stored within your abdominal cavity. Visceral fat is dangerous because it tends to lodge around your organs. Fat around your abdomen can fuel insulin resistance and inflammation and is believed to be the leading cause of chronic illnesses.

The Ketogenic diet is very effective at reducing visceral fat, and you will notice your waistline shrinking when you start following the Ketogenic diet

3. *Increased levels of good cholesterol*

Good cholesterol is biologically referred to as High-Density Lipoprotein (HDL).

Good cholesterol levels tend to increase under the Ketogenic diet as your body carried the Low-Density Lipoprotein (LDL) or the bad cholesterol away from your body and into the liver where it is recycled and excreted as waste

4. *Kills Your Appetite.*

Hunger and deprivation are the worst side effects of any diet, and this is one of the main reasons why most diets fail. But not the Keto diet.

By cutting carbs and replacing them with healthy fats and protein, your body will take more time to digest fats and proteins than it did carbs and you will naturally eat less. In the end, you'll stay full longer and lose more weight!

5. *Reduced symptoms of type 2 diabetes*

When you eat a lot of carbs, your body breaks them down into simple sugars. Once this glucose gets into your bloodstream, it elevates your blood sugar levels and triggers the release of insulin. The release of insulin instructs your cells to take in the glucose and use it, or store it as fat for later use,

Continued intake of low-quality carbs, such as white bread or sweetened beverages, can lead to insulin resistance. When this happens, your cells are not able to recognize insulin, and it becomes harder for your body to take the blood sugar into your cells. This is what leads to type 2 diabetes.

Reversing this cycle requires one to cut carbs from their diet to the point where the body doesn't need to release high amounts of insulin.

Benefits of Keto Diet

The list of health benefits secured from a Keto Diet will never be ending. Nevertheless, for your convenience, a few of the more significant health benefits that you can gain from a Keto Diet will be explained.

- **Epilepsy**: Since the Ketogenic diet is a diet that features high fat, low carbohydrate, and controlled consumption of protein, it causes the body to use fat as the primary energy source energy. In a lot of epileptic cases, switching to a Ketogenic diet has resulted in a lowered incidence of seizures. Exercise care and supervision when children are following the diet.

- **Reversing Type 2 Diabetes**: This is one of the benefits of being on a Ketogenic diet. There are many success stories about this diet, which research has proven is a result of lowering the amount of carbohydrate that you consume, and as a result, your blood sugar level is brought to natural homeostasis. It is important to note that carb stimulates the body system to discharge the hormone called insulin. So, when carb intake is lowered, the body does not release more insulin to control the blood sugar which will, in turn, increase the burning of fat that has been stored in the body. How then does this work in reversing Type 2 diabetes? The answer to the question is simple.

The fundamental problem faced by people with diabetes is a high amount of blood sugar that comes primarily from carb intake.

Once a person in on a Ketogenic diet, since they eat a fewer amount of carbs, the body can easily control the amount of blood sugar which has the capacity of reversing Type 2 diabetes.

- **Weight Loss**: What happens during ketosis? Your body shifts from burning carbs as fuel into burning fat which results in tremendous weight loss. As you dive deeper into the sea of ketosis, your body burns fat resulting in weight loss. Instead of other types of diets which may have been using for weight loss without success, with Ketogenic diet, you lose body fat and weight quickly.

- **Useful Mental Agility**: When ketosis mode is fully activated, there is a constant supply of ketones to the brain. Remember that when the body is not in ketosis mode and carb is steadily fed into the body system, the brain makes use of carb as a fuel source and many are of the opinion that to increase mental agility and focus, more carbs need to be consumed.

On the contrary, when you are entirely in ketosis, your body registers a massive change in fuel consumption, meaning it burns more fat rather than the conventional carbs, resulting in fat in your body are broken down into ketone bodies. Other organs in the body can make use of fat.

However, the brain makes use of ketones broken down from fat. During ketosis, there is usually an increase in the flow of ketone bodies to the brain giving it a more active mental agility and focus.

- **Acne Reduction**: It has been reported with the colossal success that many people who have acne problems when on low carb diets like the Ketogenic diet, their acne is drastically reduced. When on a Ketogenic diet the intake of carb is lowered. Where carbs are consumed, the body needs to produce the hormone called insulin to reduce the amount of blood sugar in the bloodstream. Acne is mostly caused and driven by insulin. It is the cornerstone of acne. Besides acting as the primary agent that motivate skin cells to manufacture sebum (an oily secretion secreted by the sebaceous gland for lubricating the hair and skin and protects against bacteria) and keratin (a fibrous insoluble protein that is the primary structural element in hair and nail), it heightens the secretion of many other hormones that causes acne. What does this all mean?
When you are on a low carb diet like the Ketogenic diet, the flow of insulin to lower the amount of blood sugar in your bloodstream is not necessarily needed since your body does not require that. Insulin, being one of the leading causes of acne, will be curtailed since you do not consume many carbs that will summon its presence in your bloodstream.

When there is no sugar to reduce in the blood, your insulin will not be used as often.

- **Enhanced Stamina**: While practicing the Ketogenic diet, your physical stamina and endurance will be improved since you will have access to storage of fat that your body has reserved. At a time of intense exercise, your stored carbs will melt away like the dissolving ice beaten down upon by summer light. On the other hand, your fat storage can last longer than your carbs. When you are carb adapted, your fat stores are quickly depleted during a short time of intense exercise and to refill; you must keep eating. However, when you are on a Ketogenic diet, most of the fuel that is available is fat, with more long-lasting effects than your regular carb stores. Your body and your brain are energized by your fat stores making you last longer in exercise and have more stamina than someone who is relying on carbs for their strength and endurance.

- **Enhanced Performance**: Since your body is experiencing a shift from what it is used to, it is possible that at the formative stage of the Ketogenic diet you might experience some form of reduced performance.

But will this remain for a long time? Certainly not. The benefits of going Ketogenic are more long term than short term. Today many athletes are going Ketogenic, and they have improved their performance, especially in long distance running. As I have explained earlier, your fat stores last longer than your carb stores. Since fat stores last longer, an athlete can perform for a prolonged period without refueling with external energy.

- **Decreased Aging**: With the Ketogenic diet, your body can and will look younger for longer. When you have entered ketosis, ketone bodies are produced.

These bodies may decrease the aging process by blocking a group of enzymes known as histone deacetylases. The enzymes function to keep a couple of genes known as Forkhead box O3 and Metallothionein 2A turned off. These genes can empower other cells to resist oxidative stress. The good thing is that the ketone bodies produce when full fledge ketosis has been entered can block Forkhead box O3 allowing the genes to be reactivated which prevents oxidative stress because it is this oxidative stress that indirectly causes aging. Besides, the Ketogenic diet reduces blood sugar levels. It is important to know that when sugar levels are reduced, glycation and the production of enhanced glycation by-product materials made from high blood sugar heightens tissue damage, diabetes, and aging. Finally, the Ketogenic diet is a catalyst that reduces triglycerides which are known for causing a lot of terminal diseases.

- **Alzheimer disease**: This is a mental disorder that causes dementia because of the progressive degradation of the brain. One of the features of this disease is a decreasing ability to metabolize glucose. Whenever the mind is unable to metabolize glucose, it can have a lot of adverse effects on the brain. However, with ketone bodies when a person is entirely into ketosis, the supply of ketones to the brain reduces the brain's over-dependence on glucose.

21 Days Meal Plan

Day 1
Breakfast: Savory Cheddar Pancakes
Lunch: Balsamic Herbed Pork Tenderloin
Dinner: Ginger Sesame Halibut
Snack/Dessert: Avocado Tropical Treat

Day 2
Breakfast: Chia Cinnamon Vanilla Granola
Lunch: Chicken Curry with Oil-Roasted Peanuts
Dinner: Italian Meatballs
Snack/Dessert: Cream Cheese Bacon Stuffed Jalapenos

Day 3
Breakfast: Cheese and Sausage in Portobello Breakfast Burgers
Lunch: Easy Grilled Shrimp with Avocado, Tomato, and Onion Salad
Dinner: Chicken and Sprout Bake.
Snack/Dessert: Coconut Milk Ice Cream.

Day 4
Breakfast: Cheesy Keto Quiche
Lunch: Zucchini Beef Lasagna
Dinner: Savory Butternut Squash Soup
Snack/Dessert: Choco Peanut Fat Bombs

Day 5
Breakfast: Blueberry Breakfast Scones
Lunch: Savory Beef Balls with Asian Style Dip
Dinner: Sea Bass
Snack/Dessert: Smoked Salmon and Dill Spread

Day 6
Breakfast: Keto Green Eggs
Lunch: Chicken Bell Pepper Kebabs
Dinner: Spaghetti Carbonara
Snack/Dessert: Roasted Eggplant Spread

Day 7
Breakfast: Vanilla Smoothie
Lunch: Sardine and Garden Salad
Dinner: Salmon Fishcakes
Snack/Dessert: Bacon Mozzarella Sticks

Day 8
Breakfast: Keto Mini Waffles
Lunch: Keto Squash-getti with Herbed Meatballs
Dinner: Roasted Garlic Butter Cod with Bok Choy
Snack/Dessert: Coconut Macaroons

Day 9
Breakfast: Cheddar Souffles
Lunch: Pork Salad
Dinner: Deviled Eggs with Chopped Bacon
Snack/Dessert: Cinnamon Butter

Day 10
Breakfast: Mocha Chia Pudding
Lunch: Ham, Onion and Green Bean Salad
Dinner: Low Carb Hearty Pot Roast
Snack/Dessert: Walnut Parmesan Bites

Day 11
Breakfast: Easy Scotch Eggs
Lunch: Cheesy Avocado Beef Patties
Dinner: Simple Beef Chili
Snack/Dessert: Avocado, Cream Cheese and Cucumber Bites

Day 12
Breakfast: Coconut Pancakes
Lunch: Herbed Parmesan Chicken Fingers
Dinner: Creamy Chicken Soup
Snack/Dessert: Almond Olive and Herb Tapenade

Day 13
Breakfast: Easy Breakfast Tacos
Lunch: Cheesy Sausage, Mushroom, and Spaghetti Squash Casserole
Dinner: Shrimp Tuscany
Snack/Dessert: Ham 'n' Cheese Puffs

Day 14
Breakfast: Bacon and Ricotta Breakfast Muffins
Lunch: Keto Cubano
Dinner: Bacon Burgers
Snack/Dessert: Coco Lime Fat Bombs

Day 15
Breakfast: Cinnamon Coconut Porridge
Lunch: Vegetable Wraps
Dinner: Goat Cheese and Smoked Onion Pizza
Snack/Dessert: Apple Detox

Day 16
Breakfast: Creamy Herbed-Baked Eggs
Lunch: Keto Pork and Plums
Dinner: Garlic Pork Chops
Snack/Dessert: Low Carb Guacamole

Day 17
Breakfast: Blackberry Egg Bake
Lunch: Salmon and Potato Salad
Dinner: Beef Welly
Snack/Dessert: Cauli Cheddar Bites

Day 18
Breakfast: Chocolate and Peanut Butter Muffins
Lunch: Collard Greens and Bacon
Dinner: Keto Caesar Salad
Snack/Dessert: Mango Smoothie

Day 19
Breakfast: Keto Bread
Lunch: Feta Cheese Salad
Dinner: Eggs and Bacon
Snack/Dessert: Keto Lava Cake

Day 20

Breakfast: Butter Coffee
Lunch: Chili Orange Shrimp
Dinner: Fried Cheesy Avocado Wedges
Snack/Dessert: Chocolate Coated Bacon

Day 21

Breakfast: Chocolate Chip Waffles
Lunch: Baked Chicken Nuggets
Dinner: Super Green Soup
Snack/Dessert: Raspberry Pops

Breakfast Recipes

Savory Cheddar Pancakes

Servings: 4

Ingredients:

- 4 large egg whites
- 4 oz. grated cheddar cheese
- 2 c. almond meal
- 4 tbsps. olive oil
- 1 Tbsp. chopped green onion
- 1 tsp. baking powder

Directions:

1. Combine the almond meal, water, grated cheddar cheese, green onion, and garlic in a large bowl. Mix well and set aside.
2. Whisk the egg whites in a separate bowl together with the baking powder, then add the almond meal mixture. Beat everything well until smooth.
3. Place a pancake griddle or nonstick skillet over medium-high flame and heat through. Add a bit of the olive oil and swirl to coat.
4. Once hot, ladle in an eighth of the batter into the hot skillet and cook for 1 minute per side, or until set.
5. Transfer to a platter then repeats with the remaining batter. Place in an airtight container and refrigerate for up to 3 days. Reheat before serving.

Nutritional Information:

257 Calories, 24g Fats, 2g Net Carbs, and 11g Protein.

Chia Cinnamon Vanilla Granola

Servings: 6

Ingredients:

- 56g whey protein powder
- 1 c. macadamia nuts
- ¼ c. water
- 4 tbsps. flaxseed meal
- 4 tbsps. whole chia seeds
- 4 tbsps. coconut oil, melted
- 3 tbsps. water
- 4 tsps. stevia
- 2 tsps. cinnamon
- 1 tsp. pure vanilla extract
- ¼ tsp. fine sea salt

Directions:

1. Set the oven to 350 degrees F to preheat. Line a baking sheet with baking paper and set aside.
2. Mix together the vanilla extract, water, and chia seeds in a large bowl. Set aside for 5 minutes, or until the mixture becomes gelatinous.
3. Pour the macadamia nuts into a food processor then add the flaxseed meal, protein powder, stevia, salt, and cinnamon. Pulse until the mixture is fine and the nuts are grounded.
4. Pour the gelatinous chia seed mixture into the food processor, then add about 1 ½ tablespoon of water and the coconut oil. Blend until the mixture is smooth. Set aside.
5. Using a tablespoon, transfer the mixture onto the prepared baking sheet. Then, transfer to the oven and bake for 15 minutes.
6. Once baked, remove from the oven and break into small pieces. Spread out on the pan.
7. Bake for an additional 10 minutes, or until the granola is dry and golden brown. Set on a cooling rack and allow to cool completely.
8. Transfer to an airtight container and store for up to 1 week in the refrigerator. Best served with warm milk.

Nutritional Information:

336 Calories, 31g Fats, 11g Net Carbs, and 9g Protein.

Cheese and Sausage in Portobello Breakfast Burgers

Servings: 4

Ingredients:

- 8 Portobello mushroom caps
- 8 oz. American cheese
- ¼ c. breakfast sausage
- 4 tbsps. olive oil

Directions:

1. Rinse the mushroom caps thoroughly, removing and discarding the stems and gills. Blot dry with paper towels and set aside.
2. Place a large cast iron skillet over medium flame and heat through. Once hot, add a quarter of the olive oil and swirl to coat.
3. Add two of the Portobello mushroom caps and cook for 5 minutes per side, or until browned all over. Transfer to a platter and repeat with the remaining mushroom caps. Set aside.
4. Divide the breakfast sausage into four patties.
5. Wipe the skillet clean and reheat over medium flame. Add half of the remaining olive oil and swirl to coat. Add two of the patties and cook for about 2 to 3 minutes per side, or until cooked through.
6. Add a slice of American cheese on each patty, then cover the pan and cook until the cheese is melted.
7. Slice the patties with the melted cheese into the mushroom caps. Repeat with the remaining patties and cheese slices until four patties have patties.
8. Cover the top of the mushroom caps with the other patties until you have four "burgers."
9. Wrap each "burger" in aluminum foil and refrigerate for up to 3 days, or freeze for up to 3 weeks. Reheat before serving.

Nutritional Information:

504 Calories, 41g Fats, 10g Net Carbs, 24g Protein.

Cheese Keto Quiche

Servings: 8

Ingredients:

For the Crust:
- 2 large raw egg whites
- 1 c. almond flour
- 2/3 c. dry roasted macadamia nuts
- ¾ c. extra virgin olive oil
- ½ tsp. fine sea salt

- Nonstick cooking spray

For the Filling:
- 6 large eggs
- 1 c. 36 percent heavy cream
- ½ c. mild cheddar cheese
- Sea salt

Directions:

1. Set the oven to 350 degrees F to preheat. Lightly coat a 9-inch pie pan with nonstick cooking spray and set aside.

2. Prepare the crust a day ahead by combining all the ingredients in a bowl until the mixture turns into a dough. Transfer the dough onto the prepared pie pan and spread out until completely covered. If needed, transfer to the freezer and chill for 10 minutes to set.

3. Bake the crust for 25 minutes in the preheated oven until golden brown. Then, transfer to a cooling rack and let cool completely. Cover and refrigerate until ready to cook the quiche.

4. Prepare the quiche filling by combining the eggs, cheese, and heavy cream in a large bowl. Add a pinch of salt and mix well until smooth.

5. Pour the mixture into the prepared pie crust. Bake for 25 minutes, or until the quiche is just set. Insert a toothpick in the center of the quiche; if it comes out clean, it is ready.

6. Place the quiche on a cooling rack and allow to set for about 10 minutes. Slice and serve. Store in the refrigerator in an airtight container for up to 3 days.

Nutritional Information:

166 Calories, 17g Fats, 2g Net Carbs, and 17g Protein.

Raspberries Breakfast Scones

Servings: 12

Ingredients:

- 3 large beaten eggs
- 1½ c. almond flour
- ¾ c. fresh or frozen raspberries
- ½ c. stevia
- 2 tsps. pure vanilla extract
- 2 tsps. baking powder

Directions:

1. Set the oven to 375 degrees F to preheat. Line a baking sheet with baking paper and set aside.

2. In a large mixing bowl, beat the eggs together with the stevia, vanilla extract, baking powder, and then almond flour.

3. Fold the raspberries into the batter until evenly combined.

4. Scoop the batter onto the prepared baking sheet, about 3 tablespoons per mound. Ensure there is at least 2 inches of space between each scone.

5. Bake the scones for 15 minutes, or until golden brown.

6. Transfer the scones to a cooling rack and allow to set for 10 minutes. Then, transfer to an airtight container and store in a cool, dry place for up to 3 days, or refrigerate for up to 5 days. Reheat before serving.

Nutritional Information:

133 Calories, 8g Fats, 4g Net Carbs, and 2g Protein.

Cinnamon Coconut Porridge

Servings: 4

Ingredients:

- 2 c. water
- 1 c. 36 percent heavy cream
- ½ c. unsweetened dried shredded coconut
- 2 tbsps. oat bran
- 2 tbsps. flaxseed meal
- 1 tbsp. butter
- 1½ tsps. stevia
- 1 tsp. cinnamon
- Sea salt

Directions:

1. Combine all the ingredients in a small pot and mix well until smooth.
2. Place the pot over a medium-low flame and bring to a slow boil. Once boiling, stir well and remove from the heat.
3. Divide into four equal servings and set aside for 10 minutes to thicken. Best served warm. Store in mason jars, seal tightly and refrigerate for up to 2 days.

Nutritional Information:

171 Calories, 16g Fats, 6g Net Carbs, and 2g Protein.

Easy Scotch Eggs

Servings: 6

Ingredients:

- 6 hardboiled eggs, peeled
- 1½ c. breakfast sausage
- 1½ tsps. garlic powder
- 1/3 tsp. sea salt
- ½ tsp. black pepper

Directions:

1. Set the oven to 400 degrees F to preheat.
2. Spread a large sheet of baking paper on a clean, dry surface.
3. Place the breakfast sausage in a large bowl and add the salt, pepper, and garlic powder. Mix well with clean hands.
4. Divide the breakfast sausage mixture into 6 equal balls and arrange on the sheet of baking paper. Flatten the sausage balls out, then place a hardboiled egg on top. Wrap the egg with the sausage mixture.
5. Arrange the sausage-coated eggs on a dry baking sheet and bake in the preheated oven for 25 minutes.
6. Arrange the scotch eggs on a cooling rack and let sit for 5 minutes. Store in an airtight container and refrigerate for up to 4 days. Reheat before serving.

Nutritional Information:

258 Calories, 21g Fats, 1g Net Carbs, and 17g Protein.

Easy Breakfast Tacos

Servings: 2

Ingredients:

- 2 low carb tortillas
- 4 large eggs
- ½ sliced avocado
- 2 tbsps. mayonnaise
- 1 tbsp. butter
- 4 fresh cilantro sprigs
- Tabasco sauce
- Sea salt
- Black pepper

Directions:

1. Whisk the eggs in a bowl until smooth. Set aside.
2. Place a nonstick skillet over medium flame and heat through. Once hot, add the butter and swirl to coat.
3. Add the egg and tilt until the eggs are spread out. Cook until done, then transfer to a bowl. Set aside.
4. Warm the tortillas over a low flame, then place on a platter and spread the mayonnaise on one side of each tortilla.
5. Divide the egg between the two tortillas, then add the sliced avocado, and cilantro. Season with salt and pepper, then add the pepper sauce. Roll up the tortillas and serve.
6. To store, add lime juice all over the avocado first before placing in the tortilla. Wrap tightly in aluminum foil and store in the freezer for up to 1 day. Reheat in a toaster oven before serving.

Nutritional Information:

289 Calories, 27g Fats, 6g Net Carbs, and 7g Protein.

Bacon and Ricotta Breakfast Muffins

Servings: 6

Ingredients:

- 2 large eggs
- 1 lb. ricotta cheese
- 10 oz. baby spinach, rinsed and drained thoroughly
- 7 oz. bacon
- 2 oz. chopped toasted pine nuts
- 1 c. freshly grated Parmesan cheese
- ½ c. thick plain Greek yogurt
- Sea salt
- Black pepper
- Nonstick cooking spray

Directions:

1. Set the oven to 350 degrees F to preheat. Lightly coat a 12 cup muffin tin with nonstick cooking spray and set aside.
2. Bring a saucepan of water to a boil, then add the spinach and blanch for 30 minutes, or until wilted. Drain well and set aside in a colander.
3. Meanwhile, dice the bacon and set aside.
4. Once the spinach is drained, finely chop then transfer to a large bowl. Add the ricotta cheese, pine nuts, Parmesan cheese, yogurt, eggs, and bacon. Mix very well until evenly combined.
5. Divide the mixture among the muffin cups, then bake for 30 minutes or until golden brown.
6. Place on a cooling rack and allow to cool slightly. Store in an airtight container and refrigerate for up to 3 days, or freeze for up to 3 weeks. Reheat in the microwave before serving.

Nutritional Information:

440 Calories, 29g Fats, 22g Net Carbs, 27g Protein.

Keto Mini Waffles

Servings: 8

Ingredients:

- 2 large eggs
- ½ c. almond flour
- 4 tbsps. full-fat sour cream
- 2 tbsps. melted grass-fed butter
- 4 tsps. arrowroot flour
- 2 tsps. cider vinegar
- 1½ tsps. stevia
- ¼ tsp. baking powder
- ¼ tsp. baking soda
- 1/8 tsp. xanthan gum
- 1/8 tsp. fine sea salt

Directions:

1. Combine the sour cream, egg, and vinegar with the melted butter in a bowl. Mix well.
2. Sift the dry ingredients into the sour cream and egg mixture. Then, stir gently until smooth.
3. Preheat a mini-waffle iron set on low. Once hot, cook the batter into 8 mini-waffles (or 4 regular-sized waffles) until firm.
4. Transfer to a tray and serve warm. May be stored in the freezer for up to 2 weeks. Reheat in the waffle iron before serving.

Nutritional Information:

49 Calories, 4g Fats, 2g Net Carbs, and 1g Protein.

Creamy Herbed-Baked Eggs

Servings: 4

Ingredients:

- 4 large eggs
- 60 grams 36 percent heavy cream
- 2 tbsps. grass-fed butter, at room temperature
- 4 tsps. chopped fresh parsley
- 4 tsps. chopped fresh chives
- Sea salt
- Black pepper

Directions:

1. Set the oven to 350 degrees F to preheat. Use 1 tablespoon of butter to coat four 1-cup ovenproof ramekins.
2. Crack an egg into each ramekin, then divide the heavy cream among them. Top with the fresh parsley and chives. Season with salt and pepper.
3. Arrange the ramekins on a baking sheet and bake for 20 minutes, or until the eggs are set.
4. Transfer to a cooling rack and let stand for 5 minutes before serving. To store, cover with aluminum foil and refrigerate for up to 2 days. Reheat in the microwave before serving.

Nutritional Information:

158 Calories, 16g Fats, 1g Net Carbs, and 3g Protein.

Keto Bread

Servings: 6

Ingredients:

- 3 large eggs
- 1/3 c. full fat cream cheese, at room temperature
- 4½ tbsps. flaxseed meal
- 3 tbsps. melted coconut oil
- 6 tsps. psyllium powder

- 3 tsps. coconut flour
- 3 tsps. cider vinegar
- 3 tsps. warm water
- 2¼ tsps. stevia
- 1/3 tsp. baking soda
- 1/3 tsp. baking powder
- 1/6 tsp. xanthan gum
- 1/6 tsp. fine sea salt

Directions:

1. Set the oven to 350 degrees F to preheat. Cover a baking sheet with baking paper and set aside.
2. Mix together all the dry ingredients in a bowl very well, then set aside.
3. In a separate bowl, whisk together all the wet ingredients. Then, gradually mix in the dry ingredients until smooth.
4. Divide the mixture into six equal sized rolls then arrange on the prepared baking sheet. Cover with a clean kitchen towel and let rise for about 30 minutes to an hour.
5. Once the rolls have risen to double their size, bake the rolls for 40 minutes. Insert a toothpick in the center of one roll; if it comes out clean, it is ready.
6. Transfer the rolls on a cooling rack and allow to cool slightly. Best served right away. May be stored for up to 3 days in an airtight container away from direct sunlight.

Nutritional Information:

106 Calories, 9g Fats, 4g Net Carbs, and 4g Protein.

Vanilla Smoothie

Servings: 1

Ingredients:

- Whipped cream
- 3 drops Liquid Stevia
- ¼ tsp. Vanilla
- 4 Ice cubes
- ¼ c. Water
- ½ c. Mascarpone cheese
- 2 Egg yolks

Directions:

1. Take out your blender and add in all the ingredients.
2. Place the lid on top and blend. When the ingredients are well mixed, pour into a glass and serve.

Nutritional Information:

650 Calories, 64g Fats, 4g Net Carbs, and 12g Protein.

Blackberry Egg Bake

Servings: 4

Ingredients:

- 1 tsp. Chopped rosemary
- ½ tsp. Orange zest
- Salt
- ¼ tsp. Vanilla
- 1 tsp. Grated ginger
- 3 tbsps. Coconut flour
- 1tbsp. Butter
- 5 Egg
- ½ c. Blackberries

Directions:

1. Allow the oven to heat up to 350 degrees F. Take out a blender and add all the ingredients inside to blend well.
2. Pour this into each muffin cup and then add the blackberries on top. Place into the oven to bake.
3. After 15 minutes, take the dish out and store!

Nutritional Information:

144 Calories, 10g Fats, 2g Net Carbs, 8.5g Protein.

Coconut Pancakes

Servings: 2

Ingredients:

- 4 tbsps. Maple syrup
- ¼ c. Shredded coconut
- Salt
- ½ tbsp. Erythritol
- 1 tsp. Cinnamon
- 1tbsp. Almond flour
- 2 oz. Cream cheese
- 2 Eggs

Directions:
1. Beat the eggs together before adding in the almond flour and cream cheese.
2. Now add in the rest of the ingredients and stir until well combined.
3. Take out a frying pan and fry the pancakes on both sides. Add to a plate and sprinkle some coconut on top.

Nutritional Information:
575 Calories, 51g Fats, 3.5g Net Carbs, 19g Protein.

Chocolate Chip Waffles

Servings: 2

Ingredients:

- ½ c. Maple syrup
- 50g Cacao Nibs
- Salt
- 2 tbsps. Butter
- 2 Separated eggs
- 2 scoop Protein powder

Directions:

1. Take out a bowl and beat the egg whites until soft peaks form. In a second bowl mix the butter, protein powder, and egg yolks.
2. Now fold the egg whites into this mixture and add the cacao nibs and salt.
3. Pour the mixture into a waffle maker and let it cook until golden brown on both sides. Serve with maple syrup.

Nutritional Information:

400 Calories, 26g Fats, 4.5g Net Carbs, 34g Protein.

Chocolate and Peanut Butter Muffins

Servings: 6

Ingredients:

- 2 Eggs
- 1/3 c. Almond milk
- 1/3 c. Peanut butter
- Salt
- 1 tsp. Baking powder
- ½ c. Erythritol
- 1 c. Almond flour

Directions:

1. Bring out a bowl and mix the salt, powder, erythritol, and almond flour to,....er. Add the eggs, almond milk, and peanut butter next.
2. Finally, mix in the cacao nibs before pouring this into a muffin tin.
3. Allow the oven to heat up to 350 degrees F. Place the muffin tray into the oven to bake.
4. After 25 minutes, the muffins are done, and you can store.

Nutritional Information:

265 Calories, 20.5g Fats, 2g Net Carbs, 7.5g Protein.

Butter Coffee

Servings: 1

Ingredients:

- 1 tbsp. Coconut oil
- 1 tbsp. Butter
- 2 tbsps. Coffee
- 1 c. Water

Directions:

1. Bring out a pan and boil the water inside. When the water is boiling, add in the coffee, coconut oil, and butter.
2. Once these are all melted and hot, pour into a cup through a strainer and enjoy.

Nutritional Information:

230 Calories, 25g Fats, 0g Net Carbs, and 0g Protein.

Mocha Chia Pudding

Servings: 2

Ingredients:

- 2 tbsps. Cacao Nibs
- 1 tbsp. Swerve
- 1 tbsp. Vanilla
- 1/3 c. Coconut cream
- 55 g Chia seeds
- 2 c. Water
- 2 tbsps. Herbal coffee

Directions:

1. Brew the herbal coffee with some hot water until the liquid is reduced by half. Strain the coffee before mixing in with the vanilla, swerve, and coconut cream.
2. Add in the chia seeds and cacao nibs net. Pour into some cups and place in the fridge for 30 minutes before serving.

Nutritional Information:

257 Calories, 20.25g Fats, 2.25g Net Carbs, 7gProtein.

Keto Green Eggs

Servings: 2

Ingredients:

- ¼ tsp. Ground cayenne
- ¼ tsp. Ground cumin
- 4 Eggs
- ½ c. Chopped parsley
- ½ c. Chopped cilantro
- 1 tsp. Thyme leaves
- 2 Garlic Cloves
- 1 tbsp. Coconut oil
- 2 tbsps. Butter

Directions:
1. Melt the butter and coconut oil in a skillet before adding the garlic and frying.
2. Add in the thyme, parsley, and cilantro and cook another 3 minutes.
3. At this time, add in the eggs and season. Cover with a lid and let this cook for another 5 minutes before serving.

Nutritional Information:
311 Calories, 27g Fats, 4g Net Carbs, and 12.8 Protein.

Cheddar Souffles

Servings: 8

Ingredients:

- 2 c. Cheddar cheese
- ¾ c. Heavy cream
- ¼ tsp. Cayenne pepper
- ½ tsp. Xanthan gum
- ½ tsp. Pepper
- 1 tsp. Ground mustard
- 1 tsp. Salt
- ½ c. Almond flour
- Salt
- ¼ tsp. tartar cream
- 6 Eggs
- ¼ c. Chopped chives

Directions:

1. Allow the oven to heat up to 350 degrees F. Take out a bowl and mix all the ingredients besides the eggs and cream of tartar together.
2. Separate the egg whites and yolks and add the yolks in with the first mixture. Beat the egg whites and cream of tartar until you get stiff peaks to form.
3. Take this mixture and add into the other mixture. When done, pour into the ramekins and place in the oven.
4. After 25 minutes, these are done, and you can serve or store.

Nutritional Information:

288 Calories, 21g Fats, 3g Net Carbs, and 14g Protein.

Ricotta Pie

Servings: 6

Ingredients:

- 1 c. Mozzarella
- 3 Eggs
- 2 c. Ricotta cheese
- 8 c. Swiss chard
- 1 Garlic clove
- ½ c. Chopped onion
- 1 tbsp. Olive oil
- 1 lb. Mild sausage
- Pepper
- Salt
- Nutmeg
- ¼ c. Parmesan

Directions:

1. Heat up the garlic, onion, and oil on a pan. When those are warm, add in the Swiss chard and fry to make the leaves wilt.

2. Add in the nutmeg and set it aside. In a new bowl, beat the eggs before adding in the cheeses. Now add in the prepared Swiss chard mixture.

3. Roll out the sausage and press it into a pie tart. Pour the filling inside. Allow the oven to heat to 350 degrees F.

4. Place the pie inside and let it bake. After 30 minutes, it is done, and you can store or serve.

Nutritional Information:

344 Calories, 27g Fats, 4g Net Carbs, and 23g Protein.

Lunch Recipes

Savory Beef Balls with Asian Style Dip

Servings: 5

Ingredients:

- 1 lb. organic ground beef
- 1 large egg
- 1 minced red onion
- 2 minced garlic cloves
- ½ tsp. sea salt
- Black pepper

For the Sauce:

- 1 minced garlic clove
- ¼ c. light soy sauce
- 2 tbsps. rice wine vinegar
- 1 tbsps. grated ginger
- 1 tbsp. chopped green onion
- Liquid Stevia
- Nonstick cooking spray

Directions:

1. Set the oven to 425 degrees F to preheat. Lightly coat a baking sheet with nonstick cooking spray and set aside.
2. Place the ground beef in a large mixing bowl and add the egg, onion, salt, garlic, and a generous pinch of black pepper. Mix everything well with clean hands.
3. Make about 40 1-inch sized balls from the meat mixture and arrange them on the prepared baking sheet.
4. Bake the meatballs in the preheated oven for about 12 minutes, or until browned all over but still moist.
5. While the meatballs are cooking, combine all the sauce ingredients in a dipping bowl and stir well.
6. Once the meatballs are cooked, transfer them to an airtight container and allow to cool slightly before sealing. Store the dipping sauce in a separate airtight container.
7. Refrigerate the meatballs and sauce for up to 3 days, or freeze for up to 3 weeks. Reheat before serving.

Nutritional Information:

238 Calories, 14g Fats, 3g Net Carbs, and 24g Protein.

Chicken Curry with Oil-Roasted Peanuts

Servings: 3

Ingredients:

- 1 minced garlic clove
- 7½ oz. full-fat unsweetened coconut milk
- ½ lb. chicken breast
- ¼ c. diced yellow onion
- ¼ c. water
- ¼ c. oil roasted peanuts
- 2 tbsps. chopped fresh cilantro
- 1½ tbsps. melted coconut oil
- 1½ tbsps. melted palm oil
- ½ tbsp. curry powder
- 1 tsp. minced fresh ginger
- Sea salt
- Red pepper flakes

Directions:

1. Place a saucepan over medium flame and add the coconut and palm oil. Swirl to combine.
2. Stir in the onion and curry powder then sauté until the onions are tender.
3. Stir in the sliced chicken and sauté until the chicken is cooked through. Then, add the ginger and garlic and sauté until fragrant.
4. Add the water, and coconut milk then brings to a boil.
5. Once boiling, reduce to simmer and stir in the peanuts. Continue to simmer until the curry is thickened and the chicken is completely cooked.
6. Remove the curry from heat and stir in the cilantro. Season to taste with salt and red pepper flakes.
7. Divide between two airtight containers and allow to cool slightly. Cover and refrigerate for up to 3 days. Reheat before serving.

Nutritional Information:

586 Calories, 56g Fats, 6g Net Carbs, and 18g Protein.

Zucchini Beef Lasagna

Servings: 10

Ingredients:

- 2 large zucchinis
- 1 large yellow onion, chopped
- 2 minced garlic cloves
- 1 lb. 75 percent lean ground beef
- 2 c. no sugar organic pasta sauce
- 1 c. ricotta cheese
- ½ c. shredded Parmesan cheese
- 8 tbsps. shredded mozzarella cheese
- 2 tbsps. chopped fresh oregano
- 2 tbsps. olive oil
- 1 tbsp. chopped fresh basil
- ¼ tsp. fine sea salt
- ¼ tsp. black pepper

Directions:

1. Set the oven to 375 degrees F to preheat.
2. Place a saucepan over medium-high flame and heat through. Once hot, add the olive oil and swirl to coat.
3. Sauté the onion in the saucepan until tender, then stir in the garlic and sauté until fragrant.
4. Add the ground beef to the saucepan and stir, breaking up, until browned all over.
5. Stir in the pasta sauce then bring to a simmer. Once simmering, reduce to low flame and stir in the basil, oregano, and salt. Mix well then set aside.
6. Halve the zucchinis lengthwise, then slice into extra thin strips, about 1/8 inch thick.
7. Arrange 6 zucchini slices on the bottom of the baking dish, then add a quarter of the meat sauce on top. Add ¼ cup of the ricotta cheese with 2 tablespoons of mozzarella cheese. Repeat, ensuring the zucchini slices crisscross.
8. Once the lasagna is assembled, top with Parmesan cheese and black pepper. Bake in the oven for 1 hour, or until the top is browned and bubbling.
9. Carefully remove the lasagna from the oven and place on the kitchen counter. Allow to set for about 15 minutes, then slice into 10 equal servings.
10. Allow to cool slightly, then cover and refrigerate for up to 4 days. Reheat before serving.

Nutritional Information:

366 Calories, 15g Fats, 12g Net Carbs, 46g Protein.

Chicken Bell Pepper Kebabs

Servings: 4

Ingredients:

- 2 lbs. boneless and skinless chicken breasts
- 3 crushed garlic cloves
- 1 sliced red bell pepper
- 1 sliced green bell pepper
- ¾ c. olive oil
- 2½ tbsps. squeezed lemon juice
- 1 tbsp. chopped fresh parsley
- 2½ tsps. grated lemon zest
- Sea salt
- Black pepper

Directions:

1. If using wooden skewers, then soak in ice water.
2. Rinse the chicken breasts thoroughly then blot dry with paper towels and set aside.
3. Chop the chicken breasts into bite-sized chunks then set aside.
4. Combine ¼ cup of the olive oil with the crushed garlic and lemon zest. Mix well, then stir in the parsley with a pinch of salt and pepper. Mix well.
5. Place the chicken cubes into the mixture and toss several times to coat. Once mixed, cover and refrigerate for up to 12 hours to marinate.
6. Once ready to cook, combine the remaining olive oil with the lemon juice then season to taste with salt and pepper.
7. Set the broiler or grill to medium to preheat.
8. Skewer the chicken and bell peppers, alternating the three. Then, coat the kebabs in the lemon and olive oil mixture.
9. Broil the skewered chicken and pepper for 10 minutes, turning and basting occasionally. Once the chicken is cooked, and the bell peppers are browned, transfer to a platter.
10. Allow the chicken and bell pepper kebabs to cool slightly, then store in an airtight container and refrigerate for up to 3 days. Reheat before serving.

Nutritional Information:

287 Calories, 20g Fats, 4g Net Carbs, 52g Protein.

Easy Grilled Shrimp with Avocado, Tomato and Onion Salad

Servings: 6

Ingredients:

- 2 cubed avocados
- 2 lb. deveined shrimp
- ½ c. chopped tomato
- ½ c. chopped bell pepper
- ½ c. chopped onion

- 4 tbsps. olive oil
- 2 tsps. squeezed lime juice
- 1 tsp. garlic powder
- 1 tsp. fine sea salt
- ¼ tsp. black pepper

Directions:
1. Place a grill over medium-high flame and heat through.
2. Meanwhile, combine the garlic powder, half the salt and pepper, and olive oil in a large bowl. Add the shrimp and toss well to coat. Set aside.
3. In a salad bowl, combine the bell pepper, tomato, onion, avocado, and lime juice. Season with the remaining salt and toss gently to coat. Cover and refrigerate until ready to serve.
4. Cook the shrimp in the hot grill for 3 minutes per side, or until cooked through.
5. Divide the shrimp into individual servings, followed by the salad. Cover and refrigerate for up to 3 days. Reheat the shrimp before serving.

Nutritional Information:
409 Calories, 25g Fats, 11g Net Carbs, 36g Protein.

Balsamic Herbed Pork Tenderloin

Servings: 2

Ingredients:

- ¾ lb. pork tenderloin
- 1 minced garlic clove
- 1 minced shallot
- 3 tbsps. butter
- 2 tbsps. balsamic vinegar
- 1½ tbsps. olive oil
- ¾ tsp. soy sauce
- 3 fresh rosemary sprigs
- 3 fresh thyme sprigs
- Sea salt
- Black pepper

Directions:
1. Set the oven to 475 degrees F to preheat.
2. Blot the pork medallions dry with paper towels then season with salt and pepper.
3. Place an ovenproof skillet over medium-high flame and heat through. Once hot, add the olive oil and ¾ tablespoon of butter then swirl to coat.
4. Add the garlic and shallot then sauté until fragrant. Add the pork medallions and sear for 2 minutes per side.
5. Stir in the balsamic vinegar, soy sauce, thyme, rosemary, and remaining butter. Stir well to combine, then spoon the mixture over the pork.
6. Simmer for 2 minutes, then bake for 5 minutes.
7. After 5 minutes, turn over the pork medallions and cook for an added 5 minutes, or until the internal temperature of the pork is 150 degrees F.
8. Transfer the pork to a platter and let rest for 3 minutes. Then, divide into individual servings and spoon the sauce on top. Cover and refrigerate for up to 3 days.

Nutritional Information:
508 Calories, 34g Fats, 4g Net Carbs, 45g Protein.

Keto Squash-getti with Herbed Meatballs

Servings: 6

Ingredients:

- 1 extra large or 2 medium spaghetti squash
- ¾ c. chopped fresh parsley
- 4½ tbsps. water
- 3 tbsps. olive oil
  For the Herbed Meatballs:
- 2 minced garlic cloves
- ¾ lb. lean ground beef

- ¾ lb. ground pork
- 1½ c. organic pasta sauce, no sugar added
- ¾ c. shredded Parmesan cheese
- 3 tbsps. chopped oregano
- 3 tbsps. chopped fresh basil
- ¾ tsp. onion powder
- 1/3 tsp. fine sea salt
- 1/3 tsp. black pepper

Directions:

1. Halve the spaghetti squash lengthwise. Scoop out and discard the seeds, then place on a microwaveable dish, cut side face down. Microwave for 12 minutes on high.
2. Carefully scoop out the squash mixture from the shells using a large fork and transfer to a bowl.
3. Place a skillet over medium-high flame and heat through. Add 1 ½ tablespoon of olive oil and swirl to coat.
4. Add the squash and stir well until browned. Transfer to a bowl and fold in 1/3 cup of parsley. Set aside.
5. Pour the remaining parsley in a large bowl, then mix in the pork, beef, oregano, basil, garlic, onion powder, 1/3 cup of the Parmesan cheese, and salt and pepper. Mix well with clean hands.
6. Divide the mixture into 18 equal sized balls, then arrange on a platter.
7. Place a heavy-duty skillet over medium-high flame and heat through. Once hot, add the remaining olive oil and swirl to coat.
8. Cook the meatballs, in batches, if needed, for 2 minutes per side, or until cooked through.
9. Once all the meatballs are cooked, return them all to the skillet and add the pasta sauce. Bring to a simmer, then stir and reduce to low flame. Simmer for 15 minutes.

10. Divide the spaghetti squash into individual servings then divide the meatballs as well Sprinkle with the remaining Parmesan cheese then let cool slightly. Cover and refrigerate for up to 3 days. Reheat before serving.

Nutritional Information:

460 Calories, 28g Fats, 11g Net Carbs, 43g Protein.

Sardine and Garden Salad

Servings: 3

Ingredients:

- 1 diced cucumber
- 2 diced tomatoes
- 1 minced red onion
- 2 chopped sardine fillets
- 2 c. chopped arugula leaves
- ¼ c. chopped fresh flat leaf parsley

For the dressing:

- 2 tbsps. extra virgin olive oil
- ½ tbsp. squeezed lemon juice
- Sea salt
- Black pepper

Directions:

1. Combine the ingredients for the dressing in a bowl and set aside.
2. Toss together the chopped sardines, vegetables, and herbs in a bowl. Mix well, then divide into individual servings.
3. Divide the whole sardine fillets among the servings.
4. Drizzle the dressing over the salads, then cover and refrigerate for up to 3 days.

Nutritional Information:

150 Calories, 11g Fats, 8g Net Carbs, and 6g Protein.

Herbed Parmesan Chicken Fingers

Servings: 6

Ingredients:

- 2 lbs. boneless and skinless chicken breast
- 4 chopped garlic cloves
- 4 oz. butter
- 1 c. grated Parmesan cheese
- 2 tbsps. chopped fresh thyme
- 1 tsp. chili pepper flakes
- Sea salt
- Black pepper
- Nonstick cooking spray

Directions:

1. Set the oven to 350 degrees F to preheat. Lightly coat a baking sheet with nonstick cooking spray and set aside.
2. Place a saucepan over medium flame and heat through. Add the butter and swirl to melt.
3. Stir the garlic into the saucepan and sauté until fragrant. Remove from heat and set aside for 15 minutes.
4. Combine the thyme, Parmesan cheese, chili pepper, and a pinch of salt and pepper. Stir well to combine then set aside.
5. Rinse the chicken breast thoroughly then blot dry with paper towels. Slice into 24 fingers, then coat in the garlic butter mixture.
6. Dredge the chicken fingers in the cheesy mixture then arrange on the prepared baking sheet.
7. Bake for 25 to 30 minutes, or until the chicken fingers are golden brown and cooked through.
8. Transfer the chicken fingers to a cooling rack and allow to cool completely. Store in an airtight container and refrigerate for up to 3 days. Reheat before serving.

Nutritional Information:

370 Calories, 20g Fats, 6g Net Carbs, 40g Protein.

Ham, Onion and Green Bean Salad

Servings: 3

Ingredients:

- ½ lb. trimmed green beans
- 1 minced white onion
- 1 diced roasted red bell pepper
- 1 oz. chopped Spanish ham
- 1 chopped hardboiled egg
- 2½ tbsps. fresh flat leaf parsley
- 2 tbsps. extra virgin olive oil
- 1½ tbsps. red wine vinegar
- Sea salt
- Black pepper

Directions:
1. Rinse and drain the steamed green beans. Blot dry with paper towels and set aside.
2. Combine the olive oil, vinegar, and a dash of salt and pepper. Mix well.
3. Divide the green beans into individual servings, followed by the minced onion, ham, peppers, egg, and parsley. Add the dressing.
4. Cover and refrigerate for up to 2 days. Reheat before serving, if desired.

Nutritional Information:
102 Calories, 8g Fats, 5g Net Carbs, and 4g Protein.

Cheesy Avocado Beef Patties

Servings: 2

Ingredients:

- ½ lb. 85 percent lean ground beef
- 1 small avocado
- 2 slices yellow cheddar cheese
- Sea salt
- Black pepper

Directions:
1. Preheat the broiler or grill to high.
2. Divide the ground beef into two equal sized patties. Season with salt and pepper.
3. Grill or broil the beef patties for about 5 minutes per side, or until cooked through.
4. Transfer the patties to a platter and add the cheese. To store, wrap in aluminum foil and refrigerate for up to 3 days.
5. Right before serving, reheat the burger patty in a microwave oven. Slice the avocado into thin strips and place on top of the patty. Serve warm, preferably with a light, low carb salad.

Nutritional Information:
568 Calories, 43g Fats, 9g Net Carbs, 38g Protein.

Cheesy Sausage, Mushroom and Spaghetti Squash Casserole

Servings: 10

Ingredients:

- 1 large spaghetti squash
- 1 minced onion
- ½ lb. lean organic ground beef
- ½ lb. Italian sausage
- ½ lb. chicken or turkey sausage
- ½ lb. sliced mushrooms
- 18 oz. diced tomatoes

- 8 oz. grated Parmesan cheese
- 6 oz. organic tomato paste
- 4 oz. mozzarella cheese
- 4 oz. ricotta cheese
- ½ c. butter
- ½ c. red wine
- ½ tsp. sea salt
- ½ tsp. black pepper

Directions:

1. Set the oven to 350 degrees F to preheat.
2. Pierce the spaghetti squash all over with a sharp then place in the microwave and microwave on high for about 20 minutes. set aside to cool.
3. Melt the butter in a skillet over medium-high flame. Sauté the ground beef and sausages until cooked through and crumbled.
4. Add the red wine and simmer until liquid is reduced. Then, stir in the onion and garlic. Sauté until tender.
5. Add the mushrooms and sauté until tender. Stir in the diced tomatoes, tomato paste, and seasonings. Sauté until combined.
6. Halve the spaghetti squash and scrape out the flesh. Set aside.
7. Spread half the spaghetti squash in a baking dish then add 2 ounces each of the mozzarella and ricotta, followed by 4 ounces of the Parmesan.
8. Spoon some tomato sauce on top, then add the remaining spaghetti squash. Add the remaining cheeses, then cover the dish.
9. Bake for 20 minutes, then uncover and bake for an additional 20 minutes.
10. Set the oven to broil and broil the casserole for 3 minutes, or until the top is browned and crisp.
11. Place on a cooling rack and let sit for 15 minutes. Slice into 10 equal servings, then cover and

refrigerate for up to 5 days. Reheat befor
serving.

Nutritional Information:

402 Calories, 24g Fats, 15g Net Carbs, 31g Protein.

Keto Cubano

Servings: 4

Ingredients:

- Bib lettuce
- 2 tbsps. Dijon mustard
- 2 tbsps. Mayo
- 1 tbsp. Melted butter
- ¼ lb. Sliced Swiss cheese
- 1/3 lb. Cooked pork tenderloin
- 1/3 lb. Sliced cooked ham
- Sliced dill pickles

Directions:
1. Mix together the mustard and the mayo and spread over the lettuce.
2. Divide up the meats, cheese, and pickle between the sandwiches and roll them up tightly.
3. Serve right away.

Nutritional Information:
472 Calories, 36g Fats, 7g Net Carbs, and 28g Protein.

Pork Salad

Servings: 2

Ingredients:

- ½ Sliced pear
- 1/3 c. Blue cheese
- ½ lb. Pork belly slices
- 2 tsps. Olive oil
- 2 tbsps. White wine vinegar
- ½ tsp. Mustard
- 1 tsp. Water
- 1 tbsp. Stevia
- 1/3 c. Chopped walnuts
- 2 tsps. Salt
- 2 c. Salad leaves

Directions:

1. Cover the pork with half your oil and then cook it in the oven for 30 minutes.
2. Warm up a pan and add the stevia and water. When the stevia dissolves, add the walnuts and cook for about five minutes.
3. Take the nuts and allow them to cool. While those are cooling, chop the cheese and pear into smaller bits.
4. To make the dressing, add the oil, vinegar, and mustard to a bowl.
5. Take the pork out of the oven and slice into smaller bits. Toss the salad with the dressing before adding the rest of the ingredients and serving.

Nutritional Information:

1050 Calories, 55g Fats, 5g Net Carbs, 13g Protein.

Baked Chicken Nuggets

Servings: 4

Ingredients:

- ½ tsp. Dried oregano
- 1 tsp. Salt
- ½ c. Parmesan cheese
- ½ c. Milk
- 1 c. Marinara sauce
- 1 c. Almond flour
- 3 oz. Mozzarella cheese
- 1 lb. Minced chicken breast

Directions:

1. Allow the oven to heat up to 350 degrees. Coat a baking dish and set to the side.
2. Combine half the almond flour with the pepper, salt, cheese, and milk in a bowl. Add in the chicken and mix to combine.
3. Divide this into 24 balls and then dredge through the reserved almond flour.
4. Place onto the baking dish and place into the oven. Bake for a total of 20 minutes but flip around halfway through.
5. Once these are done, pour the sauce on top and then dot with some cheese. Place back in the oven.
6. After 15 minutes, take this out of the oven and serve.

Nutritional Information:

282 Calories, 12g Fats, 11g Net Carbs, 33g Protein.

Feta Cheese Salad

Servings: 8

Ingredients:

- 2 Chopped spring onions
- 50g Roasted pistachios
- 150g Feta cheese
- 1 Diced red onion
- 8 Beetroots
- 4 tsps. Balsamic vinegar
- 80 ml. Chutney
- 80 ml. Mayo

Directions:

1. Add the beetroot and water to a pan and let it boil, cooking the beetroot for 20 minutes. Wash with cold water and remove the skin before slicing.
2. Mix the beetroot and onion together.
3. Now work on the dressing. Add the balsamic vinegar, mayo, and chutney together.
4. Take out a platter and add the vegetables and pour the dressing on top. Garnish with the onion and pecans and serve over feta cheese.

Nutritional Information:

413 Calories, 31.9g Fats, 28.2g Net Carbs,7.2gProtein.

Salmon and Potato Salad

Servings: 6

Ingredients:

- 1 tbsp. Chopped parsley
- 6 oz. Salmon
- 1 chopped onion
- 1 tbsp. Olive oil
- 3 Baking potatoes

Directions:
1. Boil the potatoes and eggs together until done. While those are boiling, heat up some oil in a pan and fry the onions.
2. Place the salmon slices into a dish and put the onions on top.
3. Top with the eggs and the potatoes and sprinkle the parsley on top before serving.

Nutritional Information:
400 Calories, 30g Fats, 10g Net Carbs, 15g Protein.

Lamb Spinach Rogan Josh

Servings: 6

Ingredients:

- 1½ kg diced lamb
- 2 sliced red onions
- 1 c. Greek yogurt
- 2 tbsps. ghee
- Rogan Josh curry paste
- Salt
- Pepper

Directions:

1. Mix all ingredients together in a pot.
2. Add a little water and simmer for 4 hours.

Nutritional Information:

450 Calories, 28g Fats, 4g Net Carbs, 38g Protein.

Keto Pork and Plums

Servings: 8

Ingredients:

- 1kg pork belly
- 4 chopped plums
- 1 c. bouillon
- 1 tbsp. allspice
- 1 tbsp. cinnamon

Directions:
1. Make slices in the skin of the pork, so the flavor of the plums soaks through. Rub with allspice and cinnamon.
2. Mix remaining ingredients into a sauce.
3. Place pork in the pot. Stew for four hours.

Nutritional Information:
316Calories, 20g Fats, 10g Net Carbs, 24g Protein.

Chili Orange Shrimp

Servings: 4

Ingredients:

- 1kg peeled and deveined shrimp
- 2/3 c. cream
- 1 chipotle chili
- 1 tsp. orange zest
- Cinnamon
- 5 spice
- Salt
- Pepper

Directions:

1. Blend the half and half, chili, orange, salt, and pepper.
2. Put in a frying pan with the shrimp. Sautee 5 minutes.

Nutritional Information:

186Calories, 6g Fats, 3g Net Carbs, and 28g Protein.

Vegetable Wraps

Servings: 4

Ingredients:

- 1 head of romaine lettuce
- 2 carrots
- 1 cucumber
- 1 red onion
- 1 celery stalk
- dressing of choice

Directions:
1. Finely slice the carrots, cucumber, red onion, and celery into sticks of vegetable.
2. Divide between 12 lettuce leaves.
3. Roll up lettuce leaves and serve.

Nutritional Information:
20 Calories, 0g Fats, 5g Net Carbs, and 0g Protein.

Collard Greens and Bacon

Servings: 5

Ingredients:

- 500g chopped collard greens
- 1 chopped onion
- 1 bay leaf
- 3 tbsps. balsamic vinegar
- 1 tbsp. oil
- 1 tbsp. minced garlic
- 2 c. vegetable stock

Directions:

1. Put the onions and oil in the slow cooker on high for five minutes.
2. Add all the other ingredients.
3. Cook on low for 6 hours.

Nutritional Information:

82 Calories, 2g Fats, 2g Net Carbs, and 5g Protein.

Dinner Recipes

Deviled Eggs with Chopped Bacon

Servings: 6

Ingredients:

- 9 large eggs
- 6 chopped bacon slices
- 2¼ tbsps. mayonnaise
- 1½ tbsps. mustard
- ¾ tsp. paprika
- 1/6 tsp. fine sea salt
- 1/6 tsp. black pepper

Directions:

1. Place the eggs in a pot and add enough water to cover them by about an inch. Cover and place over a high flame. Bring to a boil.
2. Once boiling, reduce to a simmer, then simmer for 3 minutes. Turn off the heat and keep the eggs in hot water.
3. Meanwhile, place a large skillet over medium-high flame and heat through. Once hot, add the bacon and cook until crisp.
4. Transfer the bacon to a plate lined with paper towels and allow to drain.
5. Take the eggs out of the water and transfer to a basin of cold water. Once cool to the touch, carefully peel them.
6. Halve the hardboiled eggs carefully then scoop out the yolks and place in a bowl. Arrange the halves, cut side facing up, on a platter and set aside.
7. Mash the yolks together with the mustard, mayonnaise, salt, and pepper. Add 1/3 teaspoon of the paprika and mix well.
8. Dice the drained crispy bacon. Pour 1/3 cup of the chopped bacon into the bowl of yolk mixture and stir well.
9. Spoon the yolk mixture among the halved egg whites, then divide the reserved bacon among them.
10. Sprinkle with paprika and serve. Store the extra deviled eggs in an airtight container and refrigerate for up to 3 days.

Nutritional Information:

283 Calories, 21g Fats, 3g Net Carbs, and 20g Protein.

Keto Caesar Salad

Servings: 6

Ingredients:

- 12 c. chopped romaine lettuce
- 1/3 c. extra virgin olive oil
- 1/3 c. grated Parmesan cheese
- 3 tbsps. squeezed lemon juice
- 1½ tbsps. mayonnaise
- 1/3 tsp. anchovy paste
- 1/3 tsp. garlic powder
- black pepper

Directions:

1. Combine the lemon juice, olive oil, anchovy paste, garlic powder, and mayonnaise in an airtight container. Whisk well until thoroughly combined. Divide into 6 equal servings in small airtight containers and refrigerate for up to 3 days.

2. In a large bowl, toss together the lettuce and Parmesan cheese. Season lightly with black pepper and toss again to coat. Divide into 6 airtight containers then cover and refrigerate for up to 3 days.

3. Right before serving, add the dressing to the salad. Toss to coat then serve right away.

Nutritional Information:

93 Calories, 7g Fats, 6g Net Carbs, and 3g Protein.

Fried Cheesy Avocado Wedges

Servings: 4

Ingredients:

- 2 small eggs
- 1 large avocado
- 1/3 cup ground pork rinds
- 1/3 cup shredded Parmesan cheese
- 1½ tbsps. heavy cream
- 1/3 tsp. garlic powder
- 1/3 tsp. onion powder
- 1/3 tsp. fine sea salt
- 1/3 tsp. black pepper
- Sunflower oil

Directions:

1. Place a heavy-duty skillet over medium flame and add approximately 1 ½ inch of oil. Heat the oil to 375 degrees F.
2. Meanwhile, whisk the eggs in a small bowl then mix in until smooth.
3. Halve the avocado carefully then discard the stone. Scoop out the flesh using a spoon then slice into ½ inch thick wedges.
4. Season the avocado wedges with salt and pepper then set aside.
5. On a plate, combine the pork rinds, onion and garlic powders, and Parmesan cheese. Mix well.
6. Dip the avocado wedges in the egg mixture, then drain and dredge in the pork rind and Parmesan cheese mixture until completely covered.
7. Add the coated wedges in the hot oil and cook for 1 minute per side, or until golden brown.
8. Transfer the wedges to a platter lined with paper towels and let drain. Allow to cool slightly, then transfer to an airtight container and refrigerate for up to 2 days. Reheat before serving in hot oil, if desired.

Nutritional Information:

179 Calories, 14g Fats, 6g Net Carbs, and 8g Protein.

Simple Beef Chili

Servings: 3

Ingredients:

- 1 diced yellow onion
- 1 lb. ground beef
- 2 c. organic beef broth
- ¼ c. extra virgin olive oil
- 2 tbsps. flaxseed meal
- 1 tbsp. chili powder
- 1 tsp. dried oregano
- ½ tsp. cumin seeds
- ¼ tsp. garlic powder
- Sea salt
- Black pepper

Directions:

1. Place a heavy-duty pot over high flame and heat through. Once hot, add the beef and onion and sauté until the beef is browned.
2. Stir in the chili powder, oregano, cumin seeds, and garlic powder then sauté until combined.
3. Pour in the beef broth, flaxseed meal, and olive oil. Stir to combine, then bring to a boil.
4. Once boiling, reduce to medium-high flame and simmer, partially covered, for 1 hour or until the chili is thickened.
5. Remove from heat and cover. Allow to cool, then transfer to airtight containers and refrigerate for up to 3 days. Reheat and season to taste with salt and pepper before serving.

Nutritional Information:

567 Calories, 36g Fats, 18g Net Carbs, 41g Protein.

Low Carb Hearty Pot Roast

Servings: 3

Ingredients:

- 2½ lb. bottom round rump roast
- 1 small onion
- 1 large garlic clove
- 1 fresh thyme sprig
- 1 chopped turnip
- 1½ c. beef stock
- 1 c. halved radishes
- 2 tbsps. heavy cream
- 1½ tbsps. olive oil
- Sea salt
- Black pepper

Directions:

1. Set the oven to 475 degrees F.
2. Season the pork all over with salt and pepper.
3. Place a Dutch oven over a high flame and add the olive oil. Swirl to coat, then brown the roast all over and set aside.
4. Sauté the onion in the same pot until browned then transfer to the bowl with the pot roast.
5. Add the beef stock, garlic, and thyme, then mix well. Return the roast and onion, then add the radishes and turnips.
6. Place the pot, uncovered, in the oven and set it to 400 degrees F. Cook for 4 to 5 hours, or until the internal temperature of the pot roast is 130 degrees F.
7. Take the roast out of the pot and let cool. Then, transfer the vegetables and roast to a bowl.
8. Place a saucepan over medium flame and add the liquid from the Dutch oven. Stir in the heavy cream then bring to a boil. Then, reduce to a simmer.
9. Slice the pot roast thinly, then divide into individual servings. Divide the vegetables and sauce as well, then let cool slightly. Cover and refrigerate for up to 3 days.

Nutritional Information:

521 Calories, 25g Fats,6g Net Carbs, and 69g Protein.

Roasted Garlic Butter Cod
with Bok Choy

Servings: 3

Ingredients:

- 24 oz. cod fillets
- ¾ lb. baby bok choy
- 1/3 c. thinly sliced butter
- 1½ tbsps. minced garlic
- Sea salt
- Black pepper

Directions:

1. Set the oven to 400 degrees F to preheat.
2. Cut out 3 sheets of aluminum foil, each large enough to completely cover one cod fillet.
3. Place a cod fillet on each sheet of aluminum foil then add the butter and garlic. Add the bok choy, then season everything with salt and pepper.
4. Fold over the pouches and crimp the edges. Arrange on a baking sheet.
5. Bake for 20 minutes, then transfer to a cooling rack. Let cool slightly, then refrigerate for up to 3 days. Reheat in the oven before serving.

Nutritional Information:

355 Calories, 21g Fats, 3g Net Carbs, and 37g Protein.

Creamy Chicken Soup

Servings: 4

Ingredients:

- 1 diced yellow onions
- 2 c. organic chicken broth
- 1 c. diced cooked chicken breast
- ½ c. macadamia nuts
- ½ c. water
- ½ c. sliced celery
- ¼ c. diced carrot
- ¼ c. olive oil
- Sea salt
- Dried herbs de Provence

Directions:

1. Place a saucepan over medium flame and heat through. Once hot, add the olive oil and swirl to coat.
2. Sauté the onion, carrot, and celery until the onion is translucent. Then, stir in the macadamia nuts and chicken broth.
3. Bring to a simmer, then reduce to low flame and simmer until the carrot is tender.
4. Turn off the heat and allow the mixture to cool slightly. Then, blend with an immersion blender or high power blender until smooth, and the macadamia nuts are pureed. Pour the mixture back into the saucepan.
5. Add ½ cup of water into the soup and stir well to combine. Reheat over medium flame and reheat. Stir in the chicken and stir until reheated.
6. Ladle the soup into individual bowls and allow to cool slightly. Cover and refrigerate for up to 3 days. Reheat before serving.

Nutritional Information:

325 Calories, 28g Fats, 7g Net Carbs, and 14g Protein.

Ginger Sesame Halibut

Servings: 3

Ingredients:

- 24 oz. Alaskan halibut fillets
- 1½ tbsps. minced fresh ginger
- 1½ tsps. soy sauce
- 1½ tsps. olive oil
- ¾ tsp. sesame oil
- ¾ tsp. rice wine vinegar

Directions:

1. Set the oven to 400 degrees F to preheat. Line a baking sheet with aluminum foil and set aside.
2. Combine the sesame and olive oils in a bowl, then stir in the rice vinegar, soy sauce, and ginger.
3. Add the fish fillets and turn several times to coat.
4. Arrange the fish fillets on the prepared baking sheet. Bake for 17 minutes, or until done.
5. Cover each fish fillet with aluminum foil and refrigerate for up to 3 days, or freeze for up to 2 weeks. Reheat before serving.

Nutritional Information:

237 Calories, 35g Fats, 1g Net Carbs, and 33g Protein.

Goat Cheese and Smoked Onion Pizza

Servings: 4

Ingredients:

- 8 large egg whites
- 2 minced garlic cloves
- 1½ c. crumbled goat cheese
- 1 c. chopped yellow onion
- ½ c. coconut milk
- ¼ c. coconut flour
- 4 tbsps. organic barbecue sauce
- ¼ tsp. baking powder
- ½ tsp. onion powder
- ½ tsp. garlic powder'
- Black pepper

Directions:

1. Set the oven to 425 degrees F to preheat.
2. Combine the coconut flour, baking powder, and garlic and onion powders in a large bowl.
3. Add the egg whites, and coconut milk then stirs until smooth.
4. Place a skillet over medium-high flame and heat through. Once hot, add ¼ of the mixture and tilt until a flat "pizza crust" is formed.
5. Cook for 2 minutes per side, or until browned. Transfer to a baking sheet and repeat with the remaining batter.
6. Divide the barbecue sauce among the pizza crusts and top with onion, garlic, goat cheese, and a dash of black pepper.
7. Bake the pizzas for 5 minutes, or until the cheese is melted.
8. Transfer to a cooling rack and let cool. Then, wrap in aluminum foil and refrigerate for up to 3 days or freeze for up to 2 weeks. Reheat in the oven or microwave before serving.

Nutritional Information:

565 Calories, 38g Fats, 13g Net Carbs, 36g Protein.

Savory Butternut Squash Soup

Servings: 4

Ingredients:

- ½ lb. cubed butternut squash
- 1 bay leaf
- 2 minced garlic cloves
- 2 c. organic chicken broth
- ¼ c. heavy cream
- 2½ tbsps. olive oil
- ½ tsp. sea salt

Directions:

1. Place a saucepan over medium flame and heat through. Once hot, add ½ tablespoon of olive oil and swirl to coat.
2. Stir the butternut squash and garlic into the saucepan and sauté for about 5 minutes or until the garlic is lightly toasted.
3. Pour the chicken broth into the saucepan along with the remaining olive oil. Add the bay leaf, then bring to a boil. Once boiling, reduce to a simmer.
4. Simmer the mixture for about 20 minutes or until the butternut squash is completely tender.
5. Take out and discard the bay leaf, then turn off the heat and allow to cool slightly. Once cooled, blend using an immersion blender or high power blender until smooth.
6. Pour in the cream and blend again until smooth. Then, return to the saucepan and reheat over the medium-low flame.
7. Season the soup to taste with salt then divide into individual servings. Allow cooling slightly then seal tightly. Refrigerate for up to 3 days. Reheat before serving.

Nutritional Information:

136 Calories, 12g Fats, 8g Net Carbs, and 2g Protein.

Super Green Soup

Servings: 6

Ingredients:

- Pepper
- Salt
- ¼ c. Coconut oil
- 1 c. Coconut milk
- 4 c. Vegetable stock
- 2 c. Spinach
- 1 c. Watercress
- 1 Bay leaf
- 2 Minced garlic cloves
- 1 Chopped onion
- 1 Chopped cauliflower head

Directions:

1. Grease up a pan with some oil and cook the garlic and onion. When those are browned, add the bay leaf and cauliflower and cook for another 5 minutes.
2. Add the spinach and watercress and cook for a bit to wilt. Pour in the vegetable stock and let this boil. Cook for another 8 minutes.
3. Add in the coconut milk and then remove from the heat. Blend so this becomes smooth and creamy.
4. This can be frozen or left in the fridge for five days.

Nutritional Information:

392 Calories, 38g Fats, 7g Net Carbs, and 5g Protein.

Bacon Burgers

Servings: 12

Ingredients:

- Pepper
- Salt
- 1 tsp. Onion powder
- 1 tsp. Cumin powder
- 12 Raw sausage patties
- 1-inch cubes of cheddar cheese
- 12 Bacon

Directions:

1. Allow the oven to heat up to 350 degrees. Line a baking tray with some parchment paper. Add the sausage patties to this tray.
2. Add the seasonings to the sausage and then place a piece of the cheese in the middle of the patties. Wrap the sausage around the cheese into a ball.
3. Add the baking pan into the oven. After an hour, take them out and let cool down.

Nutritional Information:

250 Calories, 20g Fats, 1g Net Carbs, and 14g Protein.

Italian Meatballs

Servings: 4

Ingredients:

- 1 tsp. Dried thyme
- 1 tsp. Dried oregano
- ½ c. Sliced mozzarella
- 1 can Peeled tomatoes
- 1 lb. Minced beef
- 1 handful Basil
- 1 tbsp. Tomato paste
- 2 Crushed garlic cloves
- ½ c. diced Red onion, diced

Directions:

1. Allow the oven to heat up to 350 degrees. Take out a bowl and mix together the ground beef and herbs. Form into 16 meatballs.
2. Fry these in a skillet for five minutes to make them brown. Take a bit of the cooking juices and set to the side.
3. Add the garlic, tomato paste, onion, and tinned tomatoes into the ban. Simmer this for another ten minutes.
4. Place the meatballs into a dish and top with this sauce. Break up the cheese and spread it on the tomato sauce.
5. Cover the dish with some foil and place in the oven. Bake for 20 minutes. Take the foil off and bake a bit longer.
6. Serve with a salad.

Nutritional Information:

380 Calories, 23g Fats, 8g Net Carbs, 25g Protein.

Beef Welly

Servings: 2

Ingredients:

- ½ c. Almond flour
- 1 c. Mozzarella cheese
- 4 tbsps. Liver pate
- 1 tbsp. Butter
- 2 Tenderloin steaks

Directions:
1. Season the steaks. Melt some butter in a pan and let it heat up before adding the steaks to the pan. Sear it on all sides and then let them cool down.
2. Heat up some mozzarella in the microwave for a minute. Add in the almond flour to form a dough.
3. Place this dough between two pieces of parchment paper and then roll it flat. Place some pate on the dough and spread it out.
4. Cut the dough so that it can make a ball around the meat. Add some meat into the dough and cut it, wrapping it around the meat. Do this with the other piece of meat as well.
5. Allow the oven to heat up to 400 degrees. Place into the oven and let it bake. After 20 minutes, it is done.

Nutritional Information:
307 Calories, 22g Fats, 2.5g Net Carbs, 26g Protein.

Salmon Fishcakes

Servings: 2

Ingredients:

- 1 jar Hollandaise sauce
- Pepper
- Salt
- 2 tbsps. Chives
- ½ tbsp. Butter
- 4 oz. Sliced salmon
- 2 Eggs

Directions:

1. Take the time to hard-boil your eggs. Dice up the salmon while the eggs cook.
2. Take out a skillet and heat up some butter at high heat. Place half the salmon inside and crisp it up before setting aside.
3. Run the prepared eggs under some cold water and peel. Mash them into a fine piece.
4. Take the raw salmon and half the chives and mix with the egg, along with a few tablespoons of the Hollandaise sauce.
5. Split this into four lumps and turn into balls.
6. Mix the crispy salmon and chives together and dip the egg balls into them until coated.

Nutritional Information:

295 Calories, 23g Fats, 1g Net Carbs, and 18g Protein.

Garlic Pork Chops

Servings: 4

Ingredients:

- 1 Chopped onion
- 1 tsp. Crushed garlic
- 1 tbsp. Paprika
- 4 Pork Chops
- 1 tbsp. Chopped parsley
- ½ c. Heavy cream
- 1 tbsp. Butter
- 1 c. Sliced mushrooms
- 2 tbsps. Coconut oil
- ¼ tsp. Cayenne pepper
- 1 tsp. Salt
- 1 tsp. Pepper

Directions:

1. Mix together the seasonings with a third of the onion. Sprinkle on both chops and rub it in.
2. Heat up some coconut oil and brown the chops for a few minutes on both sides. Set them to the side.
3. Add in the rest of the mushrooms and onions and cook another four minutes to make the onions clear.
4. In a new pan, whisk the butter and cream on low heat. Place the chops into the cream sauce and cook for another five minutes.

Nutritional Information:

481 Calories, 32g Fats, 4g Net Carbs, and 15g Protein.

Spaghetti Carbonara

Servings: 4

Ingredients:

- 3 packets Shirataki noodles
- 5 oz. Chopped bacon
- 1½ tbsps. Butter
- 2 Garlic Cloves
- 1 c. Grated cheese
- 3 Eggs

Directions:

1. Melt the butter in a pan and then add the bacon and cook until crispy. Then add in the noodles and the garlic.
2. Stir the noodles as they are heating up. While those are cooking, bring out a new bowl and beat the eggs with some of the cheese.
3. Add the cooked noodles to a new bowl. Stir the egg and cheese mixture into this, watching for the sauce to thicken.
4. Top with the parsley and the rest of the cheese and enjoy.

Nutritional Information:

361 Calories, 29g Fats, 4.5g Net Carbs, 16g Protein.

Shrimp Tuscany

Servings: 4

Ingredients:

- ¼ c. Baby Kale
- 5 Sun-dried tomatoes
- ½ c. Parmesan
- 1 tsp. Salt
- 1 tsp. Dried basil
- 2 Crushed garlic cloves
- ½ c. Whole milk
- 1 c. cued Cream cheese
- 1 tsp. Butter
- 1 lb. Raw shrimp

Directions:

1. Melt up the butter in a pan and add in the shrimp. Cook for 30 seconds and then turn them around. Cook until they turn pink.
2. Add in the cream cheese and milk into the pan and increase the heat. Stir, so the cheese melts completely.
3. Add in the basil, salt, and garlic and keep cooking. Allow the dish to simmer so that the sauce can thicken.
4. Add in the tomatoes and kale and then serve.

Nutritional Information:

298 Calories, 18g Fats, 6.5g Net Carbs, 23g Protein.

Sea Bass

Servings: 2

Ingredients:

- 2 Lemons
- 1/3 c. Green olives
- 1 c. Grated cauliflower
- 1 Seabass
- Pepper
- Salt
- 1/3 c. Chopped parsley
- 1/3 c. Chopped mint

Directions:

1. Allow the oven to heat up to 400 degrees. Place some parchment paper on a baking pan and place the fish on top. Add some oil to the fish.
2. Slice the lemons and stuff into the bass along with the herbs. Place into the oven to bake for 15 minutes.
3. Chop up the olives and juice the other lemons. Take out a bowl and mix together the rest of the ingredients.
4. Serve the prepared fish with the cauliflower salad.

Nutritional Information:

380 Calories, 26g Fats, 3.4g Net Carbs, 27g Protein.

Eggs and Bacon

Servings: 6

Ingredients:

- Pepper
- Salt
- ¾ tsp. Paprika
- 1½ tbsps. Mustard
- 2¼ tbsps. Mayo
- 6 Chopped bacon slices
- 9 hard-boiled eggs

Directions:

1. Take out a skillet and heat it up to cook the bacon until crisp. Move to a plate with some paper towels to drain.
2. Halve the eggs and scoop out the yolks. Arrange the halves on a plater. Mash the yolks with the paprika, mayo, salt, pepper, and mustard.
3. Dice the bacon and then add some into the yolk mixture to stir well.
4. Spoon the yolk back into the egg whites and divide the rest of the bacon among them. Serve or store.

Nutritional Information:

283 Calories, 21g Fats, 3g Net Carbs, and 20g Protein.

Chicken and Sprout Bake

Servings 6

Ingredients:

- 500g Brussels sprouts
- 6 chicken legs or thighs
- 500g mushrooms
- 1 diced onion
- 1½ c. milk
- 1 c. cream
- Salt
- Pepper

Directions:

1. Mix the milk, cream, and seasoning.
2. Put all ingredients in an oven tray.
3. Cook at 130C for 4h.

Nutritional Information:

450 Calories, 30g Fats, 2g Net Carbs, 35g Protein.

Snacks/Desserts

Avocado, Cream Cheese and Cucumber Bites

Servings: 5

Ingredients:

- 1 large cucumber, sliced into 10 1/3 inch rounds
- 1 large avocado
- 8 oz. cream cheese
- 4 oz. red salmon, flaked
- 1 tbsp. freshly squeezed lemon juice
- ½ tbsp. chopped green onion
- Tabasco sauce

Directions:

1. Halve the avocado then discard the stone. Scoop out the flesh then place in a large bowl.
2. Mash the avocado and cream cheese together until everything is smooth. Add the lemon juice and mix well, then season to taste with Tabasco sauce.
3. Arrange the cucumber slices on a platter then divide the avocado cream cheese mixture among them.
4. Divide the flaked red salmon among the pieces then garnish with green onion. Serve right away, or store in an airtight container and refrigerate for up to 3 days.

Nutritional Information:

277 Calories, 22g Fats, 5g Net Carbs, 19g Protein.

Ham 'n' Cheese Puffs

Servings: 9

Ingredients:

- 6 large eggs
- 10 oz. sliced deli ham
- 1½ c. shredded cheddar cheese
- ¾ c. mayonnaise
- 1/3 c. coconut flour
- 1/3 c. coconut oil
- 1/3 tsp. baking powder
- 1/3 tsp. baking soda
- Nonstick cooking spray

Directions:

1. Set the oven to 350 degrees F to preheat. Lightly coat rimmed baking sheet with nonstick cooking spray and set aside.
2. In a bowl, mix together the eggs, coconut oil, and mayonnaise. Set aside.
3. In a separate bowl, combine the baking soda, baking powder, and coconut flour. Add the dry ingredients to the wet ingredients and mix well until smooth.
4. Fold the ham and cheddar cheese into the mixture and set aside.
5. Divide the dough into 18 small pieces and arrange on the prepared baking sheet.
6. Bake for 30 minutes, or until the puffs are golden brown and set.
7. Arrange the puffs on a cooling rack and allow to cool slightly.
8. Store into an airtight container for up to 5 days. If desired, reheat in the microwave before serving.

Nutritional Information:

279 Calories, 20g Fats, 3g Net Carbs, and 15g Protein.

Walnut Parmesan Bites

Servings: 10

Ingredients:

- 6 oz. freshly grated Parmesan cheese
- 2 tbsps. chopped walnuts
- 1 tbsps. unsalted butter
- ½ tbsps. chopped fresh thyme

Directions:

1. Set the oven to 350 degrees F to preheat. Line two large rimmed baking sheets with baking paper and set aside.
2. In a food processor, combine the Parmesan cheese and butter. Blend until combined.
3. Pour in the walnuts and pulse until crushed and combined with the mixture.
4. Using a tablespoon, scoop the mixture onto the prepared baking sheets, then top with chopped thyme.
5. Bake for about 8 minutes, or until golden brown.
6. Transfer to a cooling rack and let sit for about 30 minutes. Then, transfer to an airtight container and store for up to 5 days.

Nutritional Information:

80 Calories, 3g Fats, 7g Net Carbs, and 7g Protein.

Cream Cheese Bacon Stuffed Jalapenos

Servings: 4

Ingredients:

- 12 large jalapeno peppers
- 16 bacon strips
- 6 oz. full fat cream cheese
- 2 tsp. garlic powder
- 1 tsp. chili powder

Directions:

1. Set the oven to 350 degrees F to preheat. Place a wire rack over a roasting pan and set aside.
2. Put on a pair of plastic gloves.
3. Make a slit lengthways across the jalapeno peppers, taking care not to cut through. Scrape out and discard the seeds. Set aside.
4. Place a nonstick or cast iron skillet over high flame and heat through. Once hot, add half the bacon strips and cook until crispy. Transfer to a plate lined with paper towels and let drain.
5. Chop the cooked bacon strips and place in a large bowl. Add the cream cheese and mix well to combine.
6. Season the cream cheese and bacon mixture with garlic and chili powder, then mix well.
7. Stuff the jalapeno peppers with the cream cheese mixture, then wrap a raw bacon strip around each pepper.
8. Arrange the stuffed jalapeno peppers on the prepared wire rack, then roast for up to 10 minutes, or until tender.
9. Transfer the stuffed jalapeno peppers on a cooling rack and allow to cool slightly. Transfer to an airtight container and refrigerate for up to 5 days.

Nutritional Information:

209 Calories, 13g Fats, 19g Net Carbs, and 9g Protein.

Low Carb Guacamole

Servings: 6

Ingredients:

- 3 large ripe avocados
- 1 diced red onion
- 4 tbsps. squeezed lime juice
- Sea salt
- Black pepper
- Cayenne pepper

Directions:

1. Halve the avocados then discard the stone.
2. Scoop out the avocado flesh from 3 avocado halves and place in a large glass bowl. Mash well with a fork or potato masher.
3. Add 2 tablespoons of lime juice into the mashed avocado and mix well.
4. Dice the remaining avocado then place in a separate bowl. Add the remaining lime juice and toss gently to coat.
5. Combine the diced avocado with the mashed avocado, then add the chopped onion. Toss again to combine.
6. Season the guacamole with salt, pepper, and cayenne pepper then mix gently to combine.
7. Store in an airtight container for up to 3 days. Serve with carrot, celery, and cucumber sticks.

Nutritional Information:

172 Calories, 15g Fats, 11g Net Carbs, and 2g Protein.

Smoked Salmon and Dill Spread

Servings: 8

Ingredients:

- 4 oz. smoked salmon
- 4 oz. full fat cream cheese
- 2½ tbsps. mayonnaise
- 2 tbsps. chopped fresh dill
- Sea salt
- Black pepper

Directions:

1. Pour the smoked salmon, mayonnaise, and cream cheese into a food processor. Pulse until combined.
2. Pour the mixture into an airtight container and mix in the fresh dill. Season to taste with salt and pepper.
3. Cover and refrigerate for up to 3 days. Best served with carrot, celery, and cucumber sticks.

Nutritional Information:

70 Calories, 5g Fats, 2g Net Carbs, and 5g Protein.

Coco Lime Fat Bombs

Servings: 8

Ingredients:

- 1 oz. cream cheese
- 2 tbsps. butter
- 2 tbsps. coconut oil
- 2 tbsps. heavy cream
- 1 tbsps. squeezed lime juice
- ½ tsp. lime extract
- ½ tsp. liquid stevia

Directions:

1. Combine the cream cheese, coconut oil, and butter in a microwaveable bowl. Microwave for 10 seconds three times until melted.
2. Stir the mixture then add the heavy cream. Mix well, then add the lime juice, lime extract, and liquid stevia. Stir well.
3. Pour the mixture into an ice cube tray with 8 compartments. Freeze for at least 1 hour. Store in the freezer for up to 2 weeks. Serve chilled.

Nutritional Information:

81 Calories, 9g Fats, 0.4g Net Carbs, 0.4g Protein.

Choco Peanut Fat Bombs

Servings: 8

Ingredients:

- 2 tbsps. butter
- 2 tbsps. coconut oil
- 2 tbsps. heavy cream
- 1 tbsp. smooth peanut butter
- 1 tbsp. unsweetened cocoa powder
- ½ tsp. pure vanilla extract
- ½ tsp. liquid stevia

Directions:

1. Combine the peanut butter, coconut oil, and butter in a microwaveable bowl. Microwave for 10 seconds three times until melted.
2. Stir the mixture then add the heavy cream. Mix well, then add the cocoa powder, vanilla extract, and liquid stevia. Stir well.
3. Pour the mixture into an ice cube tray with 8 compartments. Freeze for at least 1 hour. Store in the freezer for up to 2 weeks. Serve chilled.

Nutritional Information:

73 Calories, 8g Fats, 1g Net Carbs, and 0.6g Protein.

Almond Olive and Herb Tapenade

Servings: 8

Ingredients:

- 2 minced garlic cloves
- 1 c. pitted green olives
- ¼ c. slivered almonds
- ¼ c. packed fresh basil leaves
- ¼ c. extra virgin olive oil
- ½ tbsp. squeezed lemon juice
- ½ tsp. drained capers
- Sea salt

Directions:

1. Combine the almonds, garlic, olives, capers, and lemon juice in a food processor. Pulse until shredded.
2. Add the basil leaves into the food processor and pulse again until combined.
3. Pour in the olive oil and add a dash of salt. Pulse again until the mixture turns into a chunky paste.
4. Pour the mixture into an airtight container and refrigerate for up to 5 days. Best served with grilled chicken tenders or pan-seared white fish strips.

Nutritional Information:

28 Calories, 3g Fats, 0.36g Net Carbs, 0.1g Protein.

Chocolate Coated Bacon

Servings: 6

Ingredients:

- 12 bacon slices
- 4½ tbsps. unsweetened dark chocolate
- 2¼ tbsps. coconut oil
- 1½ tsps. liquid stevia

Directions:

1. Set the oven to 425 degrees F to preheat.
2. Skewer the bacon in iron skewers, spreading the bacon out.
3. Arrange on a baking sheet. Bake for 15 minutes, or until crisp.
4. Transfer the bacon to a cooling rack and allow to cool completely.
5. Melt the coconut oil in a saucepan over low flame, then stir in the chocolate until melted. Add the stevia and stir well to combine.
6. Place the bacon on a sheet of parchment paper and coat in the chocolate mixture on both sides.
7. Allow the chocolate to dry on the bacon, then transfer the bacon to an airtight container and refrigerate for up to 5 days.

Nutritional Information:

258 Calories, 26g Fats, 0.5g Net Carbs, 7g Protein.

Portobello Mushrooms Stuffed with Ricotta Cheese and Spinach

Servings: 6

Ingredients:

- 6 large Portobello mushroom caps
- 3 minced garlic cloves
- 2 small eggs
- 1¼ c. full-fat ricotta cheese
- ¾ c. steamed spinach
- ¾ c. grated Parmesan cheese
- ½ c. extra virgin olive oil
- Sea salt
- Black pepper

Directions:

1. Set the oven to 425 degrees F to preheat. Line a baking sheet with aluminum foil and set aside.
2. Rinse and clean the Portobello mushroom caps thoroughly until all the dirt is washed off. Discard the gills and stems, then blot the mushroom caps with paper towels.
3. Season the inside of the mushroom caps with salt and pepper, then arrange on the prepared baking sheet.
4. Bake the mushroom caps for 15 minutes.
5. Meanwhile, combine the rest of the ingredients in a large bowl until completely combined. Set aside.
6. Remove the mushroom caps out of the oven and then divide the filling among them. Return to the oven and bake for an additional 25 minutes, or until the mushrooms are browned and tender.
7. Place the stuffed mushroom caps on a cooling rack and allow to cool slightly. Serve warm.
8. Store in an airtight container and refrigerate for up to 3 days. Reheat in the microwave oven before serving.

Nutritional Information:

239 Calories, 17g Fats, 12g Net Carbs, 16g Protein.

Cinnamon Butter

Servings: 8

Ingredients:

- ½ c. butter
- 5 drops liquid stevia
- ½ tsp. pure vanilla extract
- ½ tsp. ground cinnamon
- 1/8 tsp. fine sea salt

Directions:

1. Combine the butter, vanilla, cinnamon, salt, and stevia in a large bowl. Mix well until smooth.
2. Line a baking sheet with wax paper then spread the cinnamon butter mixture on top. Roll the paper to seal the butter mixture, then seal the ends.
3. Refrigerate the butter for 1 hour before using. Store in the refrigerator for up to 2 weeks. Best served on the Keto Bread or with celery sticks.

Nutritional Information:

103 Calories, 12g Fats, 0.1g Net Carbs, 0.1g Protein.

Roasted Eggplant Spread

Servings: 8

Ingredients:

- 1 lb. eggplant
- 2½ tbsps. chopped roasted red peppers
- 2 tbsps. extra virgin olive oil
- 2 tbsps. pine nuts
- 1 tbsp. squeezed lemon juice
- ½ tbsp. crumbled feta cheese
- Sea salt
- Black pepper
- Garlic powder

Directions:

1. Set the oven to 400 degrees F to preheat. Slice the eggplant lengthwise in half, then arrange on a baking sheet lined with baking powder.
2. Roast the eggplant for 1 hour, or until extra tender. Then, transfer to a cooling rack and allow to cool slightly.
3. Once cooled, scrape the eggplant flesh out of the skin and place in a food processor. Add the olive oil, red peppers, lemon juice, and pine nuts. Then, blend until smooth.
4. Transfer the eggplant mixture into a bowl and season to taste with salt, pepper, and garlic powder.
5. Sprinkle the crumbled feta cheese over the eggplant mixture and fold in well. Transfer to an airtight container and refrigerate for up to 5 days. Serve with carrot, celery, and cucumber sticks.

Nutritional Information:

54 Calories, 4g Fats, 4g Net Carbs, and 2g Protein.

Cauli Cheddar Bites

Servings: 6

Ingredients:

- 1 large cauliflower
- 4 large egg whites
- ½ c. grated strong cheddar cheese
- 2 tbsps. heavy cream
- 2 tbsps. butter
- Sea salt
- Black pepper
- Paprika
- Nonstick cooking spray

Directions:

1. Place the cauliflower florets into a pot and add just enough water to cover the base of the pot. Season with salt to taste.

2. Place the pot of cauliflower over a high flame and bring to a high simmer. Cook until the cauliflower is tender.

3. Drain the cauliflower florets then transfer to a food processor. Add the heavy cream and butter then blend until the mixture becomes a thick mixture.

4. Season the mixture with salt and pepper, then set aside to cool.

5. Meanwhile, beat the egg whites until soft peaks form. Then, fold in the cauliflower mixture and mix until evenly combined.

6. Add the cheddar cheese to the mixture and fold well until combined.

7. Cover the bowl and refrigerate the mixture for 30 minutes, or until chilled.

8. Set the oven to 375 degrees F to preheat. Lightly coat two rimmed baking sheets with nonstick cooking spray and set aside.

9. Take the cauliflower mixture out of the refrigerator. Using a tablespoon, scoop the mixture onto the prepared baking sheets into bite-sized balls. Ensure there is about 1 ½ inch of space between them.

10. Bake for 30 minutes, or until the bites are golden brown and crisp. Then, transfer to a cooling rack and sprinkle with paprika.
11. Store in an airtight container and refrigerate for up to 5 days. If desired, reheat in a toaster oven before serving.

Nutritional Information:

142 Calories, 10g Fats, 7g Net Carbs, and 8g Protein.

Bacon Mozzarella Sticks

Servings: 4

Ingredients:

- 8 bacon strips
- 4 mozzarella string cheese pieces
- Sunflower oil

Directions:

1. Place a heavy-duty skillet over medium flame and add about 2 inches of oil. Heat to 350 degrees F.
2. Meanwhile, halve each string cheese to make 8 pieces.
3. Wrap each piece of string cheese with a strip of bacon and secure with a wooden toothpick.
4. Cook the mozzarella sticks in the preheated oil for 2 minutes, or until the bacon is browned and cooked through.
5. Place the sticks on a plate lined with paper towels and let drain. Transfer to an airtight container and store in the refrigerator for up to 3 days. Reheat before serving.

Nutritional Information:

278 Calories, 15g Fats, 3g Net Carbs, and 32g Protein.

Coconut Milk Ice Cream.

Servings: 5

Ingredients:

- 2 cans coconut milk
- 7 tbsps. cocoa powder
- 7 tbsps. powdered sweetener

Directions:
1. Drain the water from the coconut milk cans and reserve only the fats from the top.
2. Mix in the cocoa and the sweetener.
3. Put in a container and place in the quick freeze section of the freezer.

Nutritional Information:
330 Calories, 30g Fats, 5g Net Carbs, 10g Protein.

Coconut Macaroons

Servings: 18

Ingredients:

- 2¼ tsps. Stevia
- 1/3 c. Coconut milk
- 1½ c. Shredded coconut

Directions:
1. Combine together the ingredients in a bowl, mixing well.
2. Pack this down with some plastic wrap and then place in the fridge for a few hours.
3. Once it is chilled, scoop the mixture into balls and then place in a container to store.

Nutritional Information:
47 Calories, 5g Fats, 2g Net Carbs, and 4g Protein.

Raspberry Pops

Servings: 8

Ingredients:

- 1 tsp. Vanilla
- 4 tbsps. Butter
- 4 tbsps. Heavy cream
- 4 tbsps. Coconut oil
- ¼ c. Chopped raspberries
- ¼ c. Cream cheese

Directions:

1. Mix the butter, coconut oil, and cream cheese together. Microwave these to melt.
2. Take the bowl out of the microwave and stir around. Add in the heavy cream and fold the raspberries.
3. Stir the vanilla and make sure to combine well. Take out an ice cube tray with 16 sections and put into the freezer.
4. Let these chill until frozen.

Nutritional Information:

166 Calories, 17 g Fats, 2g Net Carbs, and 8g Protein.

Avocado Tropical Treat

Servings: 4

Ingredients:

- 1 drop Maple syrup
- ¼ c. Natural yogurt
- ½ Sliced kiwi
- ½ Sliced papaya
- ¼ Sliced banana
- ½ Diced avocado

Directions:

1. Take out a bowl and combine the avocado with the fruit.
2. When those are mixed, add in the maple syrup and the yogurt. Mix all of these ingredients together.
3. Add to a blender and puree to a paste form.

Nutritional Information:

81 Calories, 6.5 g Fats, 6.1 g Net Carbs, 1.1g Protein.

Keto Lava Cake

Servings: 1

Ingredients:

- ½ tsp. Vanilla
- 1 tbsp. Heavy cream
- 1 Egg
- 2 tbsps. Erythritol
- 2 tbsps. Cocoa powder
- Salt
- ¼ tsp. Baking powder

Directions:

1. Allow the oven to heat up to 350 degrees. While that heats up, bring out a bowl and whisk together the erythritol and cocoa powder.
2. In a second bowl, beat the egg. Add this into the erythritol mixture along with the rest of the ingredients.
3. Prepare a few ramekins before adding in the batter. Place into the oven to bake.
4. After 15 minutes, take the cakes out and let them cool down before enjoying.

Nutritional Information:

173 Calories, 13 g Fats, 4g Net Carbs, and 8g Protein.

Apple Detox

Servings: 3

Ingredients:

- 1 tsp. Honey
- 1tbsp. Flax seeds
- ½ Apple
- 1½ Chopped celery
- 1½ Chopped Kale
- 1/3 c. Ice
- 1/8 c. Almond milk

Directions:

1. Chop up the apple, celery, and kale. Add these into a blender along with the rest of the ingredients.
2. Blend until these are mixed well, pour into glasses, and serve.

Nutritional Information:

50 Calories, 12 g Fats, 5.7g Net Carbs, 16g Protein.

Mango Smoothie

Servings: 1

Ingredients:

- 6 Ice cubes
- 1 tbsp. Sugar
- 1 tbsp. Lemon juice
- ¼ c. Vanilla yogurt
- ½ c. Mango juice
- ¼ c. Mashed avocado
- ¼ c. Mango cubes

Directions:

1. Cut the mango into cubes. Cube up the avocado as well.
2. Take out the blender and add in all of the ingredients together. Blend until smooth and then serve.

Nutritional Information:

269 Calories, 9 g Fats, 6 g Net Carbs, and 4g Protein.

Conclusion

I truly hope this book has helped you to understand and follow a specific plan while on the Ketogenic Diet. With such helpful knowledge; the next step is to try the different recipes, and enjoy the benefits of Keto diet and lifestyle. Happy Keto!

Peter Bragg

5A1 347 9631

Made in the USA
San Bernardino, CA
14 March 2019